A Book Of

BUSINESS COMMUNICATION

For
S.Y.B.Com.
As Per New Revised Syllabus, June 2014

Dr. Darekar Ramesh Dagu
Associate Professor in Commerce
K.T.H.M College Nashik.
Member of Board of Studies for BBA

Ms. Seema Pillai
M.Com., M. Phil., Master's in Management
Head of the Department of BBA &
Assistant Professor in Commerce and Management
SSR College of Arts, Commerce and Science,
Silvassa

Mr. Chetan S. Varade
M.Com., M. Phil., Master's in Management
Head of the Department of Commerce &
Assistant Professor in Commerce and Management
SSR College of Arts, Commerce and Science, Silvassa

Mr. Nikunj Bilakhia
M.B.A

N1687

BUSINESS COMMUNICATION　　　　　　　　　　　　　　　ISBN 978-93-5164-024-0
First Edition : August 2014
© : Authors

The text of this publication, or any part thereof, should not be reproduced or transmitted in any form or stored in any computer storage system or device for distribution including photocopy, recording, taping or information retrieval system or reproduced on any disc, tape, perforated media or other information storage device etc., without the written permission of Authors with whom the rights are reserved. Breach of this condition is liable for legal action.

Every effort has been made to avoid errors or omissions in this publication. In spite of this, errors may have crept in. Any mistake, error or discrepancy so noted and shall be brought to our notice shall be taken care of in the next edition. It is notified that neither the publisher nor the authors or seller shall be responsible for any damage or loss of action to any one, of any kind, in any manner, therefrom.

Published By :
NIRALI PRAKASHAN
Abhyudaya Pragati, 1312, Shivaji Nagar,
Off J.M. Road, PUNE – 411005
Tel - (020) 25512336/37/39, Fax - (020) 25511379
Email : niralipune@pragationline.com

Printed at
Repro Knowledgecast Limited
India

DISTRIBUTION CENTRES
PUNE

Nirali Prakashan
119, Budhwar Peth, Jogeshwari Mandir Lane
Pune 411002, Maharashtra
Tel : (020) 2445 2044, 66022708, Fax : (020) 2445 1538
Email : niralilocal@pragationline.com

Nirali Prakashan
S. No. 28/27, Dhyari,
Near Pari Company, Pune 411041
Tel : (020) 24690204, Fax : (020) 24690316
Email : bookorder@pragationline.com

MUMBAI
Nirali Prakashan
385, S.V.P. Road, Rasdhara Co-op. Hsg. Society Ltd.,
Girgaum, Mumbai 400004, Maharashtra
Tel : (022) 2385 6339 / 2386 9976, Fax : (022) 2386 9976
Email : niralimumbai@pragationline.com

DISTRIBUTION BRANCHES

NAGPUR
Pratibha Book Distributors
Above Maratha Mandir, Shop No. 3, First Floor,
Rani Jhanshi Square, Sitabuldi, Nagpur 440012,
Maharashtra, Tel : (0712) 254 7129

BENGALURU
Pragati Book House
House No. 1, Sanjeevappa Lane, Avenue Road Cross,
Opp. Rice Church, Bengaluru – 560002.
Tel : (080) 64513344, 64513355,
Mob : 9880582331, 9845021552
Email:bharatsavla@yahoo.com

JALGAON
Nirali Prakashan
34, V. V. Golani Market, Navi Peth, Jalgaon 425001,
Maharashtra, Tel : (0257) 222 0395
Mob : 94234 91860

KOLHAPUR
Nirali Prakashan
New Mahadvar Road,
Kedar Plaza, 1st Floor Opp. IDBI Bank
Kolhapur 416 012, Maharashtra. Mob : 9855046155

CHENNAI
Pragati Books
9/1, Montieth Road, Behind Taas Mahal, Egmore,
Chennai 600008 Tamil Nadu, Tel : (044) 6518 3535,
Mob : 94440 01782 / 98450 21552 / 98805 82331, Email : bharatsavla@yahoo.com

RETAIL OUTLETS
PUNE

Pragati Book Centre
157, Budhwar Peth, Opp. Ratan Talkies,
Pune 411002, Maharashtra
Tel : (020) 2445 8887 / 6602 2707, Fax : (020) 2445 8887

Pragati Book Centre
Amber Chamber, 28/A, Budhwar Peth,
Appa Balwant Chowk, Pune : 411002, Maharashtra,
Tel : (020) 20240335 / 66281669
Email : pbcpune@pragationline.com

Pragati Book Centre
676/B, Budhwar Peth, Opp. Jogeshwari Mandir,
Pune 411002, Maharashtra
Tel : (020) 6601 7784 / 6602 0855

PBC Book Sellers & Stationers
152, Budhwar Peth, Pune 411002, Maharashtra
Tel : (020) 2445 2254 / 6609 2463

MUMBAI
Pragati Book Corner
Indira Niwas, 111 - A, Bhavani Shankar Road, Dadar (W), Mumbai 400028, Maharashtra
Tel : (022) 2422 3526 / 6662 5254, Email : pbcmumbai@pragationline.com

www.pragationline.com　　　　　　　　　　　　　　　　　　　　　　　　info@pragationline.com

DEDICATION

This book is Dedicated To Our Honourable

Chairman Of SSR Memorial Trust

Shri Mohan S Delkar & Shrimati Kalaben M Delkar

Preface ...

A number of books are available on the subject of Business Communication in the market but they do not meet the basic requirements of B.Com students of University of Pune. This book is written as per the revised syllabus prescribed for B.Com students by the University of Pune from June, 2014. We do hope that this book will definitely help to meet the growing requirements of the students of Business Communication from the faculty of Commerce and Management. This book adopts a modern and novel approach towards the study of Business Communication in view with the specific requirements of the readers and practitioners of this subject.

Business Communication is evolving at a rapid space with the introduction of new network based collaborative technologies leading to dramatic changes in work environments. Information is now exchanged via- email; mediums are conducted through video conferencing and customer information is collected and products are promoted using the internet .Because of the various phenomenal changes in the business environment, recruiters look for students with good computers- cum-communication skills.

All socio-economic activities require effective communication skills. From preparing resumes to attending interviews, planning strategies, drafting reports etc. all call for sharpening our writing and speaking skills. This book is an effort to make students aware of the importance of developing these skills.

We are grateful to Mr. Mohan S. Delkar, Honourable Chairman of SSR Memorial Trust, for being a constant source of inspiration and encouragement in our all academic endeavour's. We thank Mrs. Kalaben Delkar, Founder and Chairman of Navshakti Mahila Mandal, for her unflinching support and guidance.

We are deeply indebted to our families whose support, insightful comments and good cheer kept us going.

We have received cooperation, assistance and suggestions from our teacher collegues, business executives and people from other walks of life. We would like to express our sincere thanks to Shri Dineshbhai Furia, Mr. Jignesh Furia, Mr. Nikunj Joshi, Ashok Bodke, Sachin Shinde, Nilesh Deshmukh, Mohsin Sayyed, Nitin Thorat, Parag Ghamandi, and their staff for the unending support and help in bringing out this book.

Authors

Syllabus ...

TERM - I

1. Introduction of Business Communication (12 P)

Introduction, Meaning, Definition, Features, Process of Communication, Principles, Importance, Barriers to Communication and Remedies.

2. Methods and Channels of Communication (10 P)

Methods of Communication - Merits and Demerits and Channels of Communication in the Organisation and their Types, Merits and Demerits

3. Soft Skills (16 P)

Meaning, Definition, Importance of Soft Skills

Elements of Soft Skills:
1. Grooming Manners and Etiquettes
2. Effective Speaking
3. Interview Skills
4. Listening
5. Group Discussion
6. Oral Presentation

4. Business Letters (10 P)

Meaning, Importance, Qualities or Essentials, Physical Appearance, and Layout of Business Letter

48 Periods

TERM - II

5. Types and Drafting of Business Letters (16 P)
1. Enquiry Letters
2. Replies to Enquiry Letters
3. Order Letters
4. Credit and Status Enquiries
5. Sales Letters
6. Complaint Letters
7. Collection Letters
8. Circular Letters

6. Job Application Letters (08 P)

Meaning, Types & Drafting of Job Application Letters, Bio-Data/Resume/Curriculum Vitae

7. Internal and Other Correspondence (12 P)
1. Office Memo (Memorandums)
2. Office Orders
3. Office Circulars
4. Form Memos or Letters
5. Press Release

8. New Technologies in Business Communication (12 P)

Internet: Email, Websites, Electronic Clearance System, Writing a Blog Social Media Network: Twitter, Facebook, LinkedIn, YouTube, Cellular Phone, WhatsApp, Voice Mail, Short Messaging Services, Video Conferencing Mobile.

48 Periods

***

Contents ...

TERM - I

1. **Introduction of Business Communication**   1.1 - 1.14

2. **Methods and Channels of Communication**   2.1 - 2.24

3. **Soft Skills**   3.1 - 3.26

4. **Business Letters**   4.1 - 4.14

TERM - II

5. **Types and Drafting of Business Letters**   5.1 - 5.56

6. **Job Application Letters**   6.1 - 6.12

7. **Internal and Other Correspondence**   7.1 - 7.22

8. **New Technologies in Business Communication**   8.1 - 8.32

***

Term - I

Chapter ... **1**

INTRODUCTION OF BUSINESS COMMUNICATION

Contents ...

1.1 Introduction

1.2 Meaning of Communication

1.3 Definitions of Communication

1.4 Features of Communication

1.5 Process of Communication

1.6 Elements of Process of Communication

1.7 Principles of Effective Communication

1.8 The Importance of Communication in the Workplace

1.9 Barriers to Communication

1.10 Overcoming the Barriers to Communication

- Points to Remember
- Frequently Asked Questions from University of Pune Examination

Learning Objectives ...

- To understand the meaning of Communication
- To learn the features, process, elements and principles of Communication
- To learn the importance, barriers to communication
- To learn the remedies to overcome the barriers

1.1 Introduction

The science of communication is almost as old as man himself. From time immemorial, the need to share or communicate has been felt. Human beings do not live in isolation. They need to communicate with each other, to understand each other's need and to express themselves. In our day to day life, we spend ample time in communicating with people. We convey thoughts, intentions, facts, ideas and emotions to the other person, and this is known as **communication**. Hence, communication is a base for all living creatures. Communication is a non-stop and two way process and there is no limit to the number of media that can be used for communication.

An organisation is a place where many individuals come together to achieve the organisational goal. An organisation is composed of separate individuals whose activities and personal goals and desires need to be coordinated, if a common goal has to be achieved. Co-ordination requires communication. For this reason, without communication an organisation, whether big or small, should have an effective communication system in place.

1.2 Meaning of Communication

The word "*communication*" is derived from the Latin word '*communis*', which means common. In its application, it means a common ground of understanding. It is a process of exchange of facts, ideas, and opinions as a means that individuals or organisations share the meaning and understanding with one another. Communication is an interdisciplinary concept because theoretically, it is approached from various disciplines such as mathematics, accounting, psychology, ecology, linguistic, systems analysis, etymology, cybernetics, auditing etc.

Communication is a process involving the sorting, selecting and sending of symbols in such a way as to help the listener perceive and recreate in his own mind the meaning contained in the mind of the communicator. Communication involves the creation of meaning in the listener, the transfer of information and thousands of potential stimuli. Communication helps us to learn, be aware of our surroundings, adjust to our environment, do important things and to grow.

To communicate with one another is a compulsive urge of human beings. Communication and mutual understanding go hand in hand; mutual understanding is the heart of human relations. Man is a communicating animal; he alone has the power to express in words. Some of the modes of exchange of messages are sight, sound, smell, touch and taste. Communication helps man to communicate effectively. Communication has made civilisation and progress of culture possible.

1.3 Definitions of Communication

- **American Society of Training Directors:** "*The interchange of thoughts or information to bring about mutual understanding and confidence or good human relation.*"
- **Leland Brown:** "*Communication is the transmission and interchange of facts, ideas, feelings, or course of action.*"

✏ **Ordway Tead:** *"Communicating is a composite of information given and received, of a learning experience in which certain attitudes, knowledge, and skills change, carving with them alternations of behaviour, of listening effort by all involved, of a sympathetic fresh examination of issues by the communicator himself, of a sensitive interacting points of view, leading to a higher level of shared understanding and common intention."*

✏ **Theo Haiemann:** *"Communication is the process of passing information and understanding from one person to another. It is the process of imparting ideas and making oneself understood by others."*

✏ **M. T. Myers and G. E. Myers:** *"Communication refers to a special kind of patterning; patterning which is expressed in symbolic form. For communication to take place between or among people two requirements must be met: (1) a symbolic system must be shared by the people involved (we need to speak the same language or jargon or dialects) and (2) the associations between the symbols and their referents must be shared."*

✏ **Chester Barnard:** *"In exhaustive theory of organisation, communication would occupy a central place because the structure, extensiveness, and scope of organisation are almost entirely determined by communication techniques."*

✏ **Simon:** *"The question to be asked of any administrative process is: How does it influence the decisions of the individuals without communication, the answer must always be: It does not influence them at all."*

1.4 Features of Communication

Some of the important features of communication have been listed below.

- **It is Unavoidable:** Since we communicate unintentionally all the time, even without the use of words, it is impossible not to communicate. Our body language, the way we dress, the importance we give to arriving on time, our behaviour and the physical environment in which we work, all convey certain messages to others.
- **It is a Two-way Exchange of Information:** Communication is sharing of information between two or more persons, with continuous feedback.
- **It is a Process:** Each message is part of a process and does not occur in isolation. This means that the meaning attached to a message depends on what has happened before and on the present context. For example, your boss's response to your request for a promotion will depend on your past relationship with him, as well as his mood at that particular moment.
- **It involves a Sender and a Receiver of Information:** Any communication starts with a sender of a message and requires a receiver to attach some meaning to that message.
- **It could be Verbal or Non-verbal:** Communication could be through the use of words in spoken or written form, or through the use of body language such as gestures and facial expressions.

- **It is successful when the Receiver interprets the meaning in the same way as that intended by the Sender:** The receiver does not always attach the same meaning to a message as the sender. When the message is wrongly interpreted, the communication is a failure.

1.5 Process of Communication

> "The ability to express an idea is as important as the idea itself."
>
> – **American businessman, Bernard Baruch**

The purpose of communication is to convey your ideas to others clearly and unambiguously. Doing this involves effort from both the sender and the receiver of the message. In this process there is possibility of error at every point because the perception of the sender and receiver about a particular message may not be the same. There should be mutual understanding between them. They should have mutually accepted set of codes in making up the common language. In fact, communication is successful only when receiver understands the same meaning as intended by the sender.

Communication takes place in a systematic process which is illustrated in the following figure.

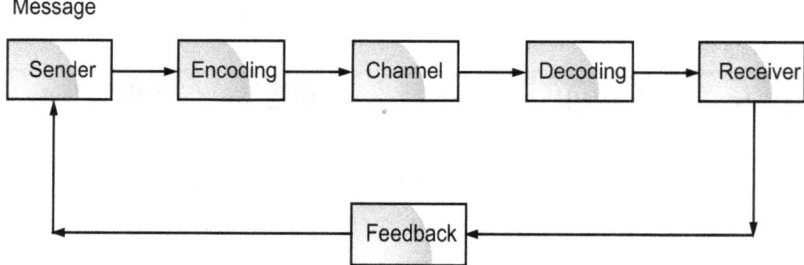

Fig. 1.1: Process of Communication

The sender, the source of information, encodes the message and sends it to the receiver through the channel (language or sign). The receiver tries to decode it. After understanding the message, the receiver acts on it which becomes the response of the feedback. The process of communication is completed when the sender gets the response from the receiver.

The various elements of communication are briefly described to understand the process of communication.

1.6 Elements of Process of Communication

1. **Source / Sender:** The communication process begins with the sender, who is the source of the message. The sender has some raw idea in his/her mind and wants to convey it for some purpose. The sender may be a speaker, a writer or an actor.

2. **Encoding:** The sender identifies, analyses and logically arranges the idea. He/ She then converts his/her idea into a language, sign, picture or gesture. He / She transforms the idea into codes which the receiver can understand. This transferring of idea into codes is called *encoding*. Here the codes or symbols are selected by the sender, keeping in mind the receiver's ability to understand them correctly.

3. **Channel / Medium:** This is the vehicle or medium which helps the sender to convey the message to the receiver. After encoding the message, the sender selects the channel or medium. The medium of communication can be written, oral or audio-visual.

Again, the written medium can be in the form of letters, memos, reports, manuals, notices, circulars etc. Similarly, the oral medium can be in the form of dialogues, interviews, telephonic conversations, conferences, recordings, etc.

4. **Receiver:** The receiver is the targeted audience of the message. He / She gets the message, understands, interprets and tries to perceive the total meaning of the message as conveyed by the sender. The receiver may be a listener, a reader or a viewer.

5. **Decoding:** The process of decoding is the exact opposite of encoding. In encoding, the sender translates the idea into codes, while in decoding; the receiver translates the codes into an idea. Decoding is the act of transmitting symbols into a meaning. If the receiver is familiar with codes more or less the same meaning will be communicated to the receiver as intended by the sender.

6. **Feedback / Response / Reaction:** After understanding the meaning, the receiver responds to the message. He /She he sends back his / her response to the sender. This return flow of communication is called *feedback*. Thus the communication process ends with the receiver putting the received message into action. The communication process is incomplete until the sender receives the feedback. Feedback is thus an indispensable part of communication process as it is the only way of getting the confirmation on the part of the sender. Feedback enables the sender to know whether his/her message has been properly understood or not.

However, in giving feedback, the receiver becomes the sender and in receiving feedback, the sender changes his/her role into the receiver. *Communication is a mutual exchange of messages*. There is no sharp difference between the roles of the sender and the receiver, because the same person plays both the roles. Thus, we see that communication completes a full circle. As a result we can say that communication is a *two – way process and a cyclic process*.

1.7 Principles of Effective Communication

Communication is a mutual, two-way and continuous social process. It should serve the organisational objectives. To achieve this, the management adopts an effective media and network of communication. To make it effective, the communicator must possess certain qualities, understand the receiver, and convey the message and see to that he acts on it.

Practical experience in the field makes both the sender and receiver to attain perfection. Communication translates organisational information into the language commonly understood in the organisation. Lack of feedback, interaction and effective decoding of signs or words into the receiver's capability are the important problems in communication. But they do not alter the basic essentials for a successful communication.

The important principles of communication are:

1. Clarity: In the communication process, message is the very subject matter of communication. Clarity of ideas, facts, and opinions in the mind of communicator should be clear before communicating. It is a thinking process to conceive the subject. The message is always subject to the test of principle of clarity. It is to be encoded in common, direct, simple and in an understandable language, so that the receiver is able to understand it without doubt and difficulty.

2. Information: Information is different from communication. All communications contain information while all information cannot communicate a message. The word *'information'* is comprehensive in which communication, is a special kind of transmitting message, in a symbolic form. The sender first collects and keeps before him the relevant information concerning a particular individual or group of people. The principle of effective communication is to have information and communicate it in a symbolic form.

3. Completeness: The subject matter to be communicated must be adequate and full, which enables the receiver to understand the central theme or idea of the message. Incompleteness of a message may result in misunderstanding the subject by the receiver. The decision-making process would be delayed and action may be delayed when the message is incomplete.

4. Emphasis on Attention: The purpose of communication is to draw the attention of the receiver. Whether the message is written or oral it should attract the receiver. To render the message attractive, it should be conveyed in a forceful, loud and clear manner, as far as is possible, having regard to the demands of the situation. The message should be systematically arranged.

5. Consistency: The message transmitted should not be contradictory. The subject matter of communication is said to be consistent when it is in agreement with the objectives and policies of the organisation. The thinking, action of happenings should be according to the same organisational rules and principles. The idea to be communicated should be in an absolutely clear, understandable, positive and precise form. The idea should not be vague and confusing. It should be easily understandable to all levels of the management. The manager should know that no communication is complete unless the message is correctly understood by the receiver in the same sense in which the communicator wanted him to understand.

Consistency can be achieved if the communicator keeps in his mind the broad objectives, policies and programmes of the enterprise. There should be some linkage and compromise between communications. One communication should not conflict with the previous communication. Conflict and inconsistency create confusion, chaos which ultimately resulting in delay in decision – making and action.

6. Integration: Achieving common goals of the enterprise is the objective of group activities. Communication as a tool of management should strengthen the enterprise. Communication is only a means rather than the end. The transmitter and receiver have to use communication tools as a means to an end, not an end in itself, so that it promotes integrated efforts of the organisation.

7. Use of Informal communication: Informal communication is called grapevine. It is a type of communication which occurs on account of informal relationship between persons. This relationship grows spontaneously from personal interest, group interest, social and other non-formal relations. Informal channel is the most effective one and transmits information with great speed. Informal organisation should be utilised properly to communicate messages. It supplements the formal communication channel.

8. Two-way Communication: An effective communication demands two-way communication. i.e. vertically, upward and downward. It should not always be downward movement from the superior to the subordinates. In such cases, communication cannot produce the desired results. The reaction and response of the receiver are equally needed to achieve the purpose of communication. A manager should not only to speak, inform, instruct, and order but should also be prepared to listen, understand, answer, amend and interpret. Thus, it involves a two-way traffic or process when the process is complete.

9. To know the Receiver: In the communication process, after transmission of the message, the receiver is the key player who has to act on the message. The receiver must understand the subject that is the main purpose of communication. While organising a message a thorough study of the receiver like his academic qualifications, technological know-how, intellectual level, status, psychological attitude etc., should be done. One cannot use the same language while communicating with an illiterate worker in a factory as one does with the Director of a company.

10. Time: The Principle aim of communication is to make the message reach at the appropriate time. It is not just the transmission of ideas, opinions etc. by the superior to the subordinate for the sake of communication. They should be conveyed at the right and proper time. Sending before time or after would not serve the purpose of communication. A delayed message is stale or historical and has no importance.

11. Simplicity: Simplicity in communication produces the best and quickest understanding and response. So, the communicator must try to achieve this principle for effectiveness. Avoid using unnecessary words, pointless prepositions, jargon etc; using familiar words is preferable. The language used should be simple and only common words should be used, which excludes using colloquial English. There is no set-rule for using familiar words. The transmitter must know the receiver's vocabulary, knowledge and understanding capacity. Simplicity is always preferable to meet all situations, because the object of any communication is to make others understand and act.

12. Communication Network: Yet another principle of effective communication is the communication network. It is the channel or route through which exchange or transmission of ideas, facts etc. flow to and from the officially designated positions in the organisational structure. Formal communication has a set network which determines the fixed route for information movement. The Network covers the downward, upward, horizontal lines of communication. In a downward line, the message moves from top to bottom and in upward line, the message moves from bottom to top. Horizontal line is for personnel in one department and personnel of equal, lower or superior position in other departments. Both vertical and horizontal lines should be used for effective communication but the distance should be less as far as possible.

13. Use of Media: There are two types of media for transmitting messages. They are oral and written media. Both have their own merits and demerits. Oral communication is more effective for certain messages and similarly written communication for other circumstances. The principle of strategic use of media is to be adopted. The need, objectives and the receiver are the factors that should be kept in mind in selecting a medium.

14. Feedback: Though the last but yet the most important key or principle to effective communication is to obtain feedback from the receiver. Knowing acceptance or rejection as to the messages transmitted is probably the most important method of improving communication. The principle of feedback promotes a two-way communication. Feedback is a process to ascertain whether or not the receiver properly understood the message. It helps you to listen, answer, interpret and amend the message. Interface and interaction are possible in feedback. It avoids errors in the transmission of message and invoking effective participation of the subordinates. Thus, feedback enables the communicator to take initiative in order to know the reactions regarding the effectiveness of communication.

1.8 The importance of communication in the Workplace

Communication is the nerve center of business today. As you go up the corporate ladder, you will find that communication skills are required more than the technical skills. Communication research has revealed that among the factors most important for managerial success, communication skills rank above technical skills. Several surveys conducted among people who have been successful in their professions have indicated that communication skills are more vital for a successful careers than subjects and professional skills learnt in college.

Communication has assumed even greater importance today, since the new model of business is based on teamwork, rather than on individual action. Teamwork requires greater coordination and communication.

Communication is also required in this age of information and technology. Without communication and human skills, technology will be of no use to an organisation as communication is needed to make sense of technology and to manage all the information. For example, communication is required to explain a new computer program or software. While computers can perform routine tasks, jobs like responding to customers' needs require a high degree of communication skills.

Effective communication serves the following specific purposes in an organisation:-

1. **Greater Awareness of Organisational Goals and Teamwork:** When there is open communication between superiors, co-workers and subordinates, there is a smooth flow of information regarding the goals of the organisation. Coordination between the different departments in particular, leads to greater motivation to work together towards achieving a common organisational goal, rather than working in isolation.

2. **Better Employer-Employee Relationships:** By listening to employees, showing empathy and giving them the freedom to express their opinions without fear of being repressed, a manager can create a climate of openness that leads to better work relationships. Employees will then feel more comfortable in approaching their superiors and discussing any matter with them.

3. **Problem – Solving:** Effective communication can help resolve conflicts between co-workers, work related and performance related problems. Face-to-face communication is especially suited for achieving this task, since it is one to one and highly personalised in nature.

4. **Improved Performance:** Effective communication by managers at the time of appraising the performance of their employees can point out areas for improvement. A constructive review of performance, through which a manager gives positive feedback and counsels the employee, instead of criticising him for poor performance, can motivate the employee to perform better.

5. **Stronger Link between Manager and the External Environment:** Apart from internal communication within the organisation, effective communication by managers with external audiences such as customers, government, bankers, media and suppliers leads to a better rapport with them. A manager will be able to understand the needs of his customers, be aware of the presence of quality suppliers of material, of the government regulations and of the expectation of the community at large, only through proper communication.

1.9 Barriers to Communication

There are many barriers to communication, an understanding and analysis of which are needed before coming up with ways to eliminate or minimise them. These barriers may be classified as follows:

1. **Environmental Barriers:** This is the same as physical noise, which could be in the form of distracting sounds, an overcrowded room, poor facilities and sound, all of which may hinder the ability to listen to and understand the message.

2. **Individual Barriers:** A major barrier to interpersonal communication is a tendency to judge, evaluate, approve or disapprove of the views of the another person. This happens particularly in situations where we have strong feelings about something. In such cases, we tend to block out the communication and form our own viewpoints.

3. **Organisational Barriers:** In organisations that are too hierarchical, that is, where there are multiple "layers", messages may have to pass through many levels before they finally reach the receiver. Each level may add to, modify or completely change the message, so much so that it becomes distorted by the time it reaches the intended receiver. In other words, there is likely to be a loss of meaning and the message may not reach the receiver in the same way as it was intended by the sender.

The following example illustrates an organisational barrier to communication.

By the time the message is passed down from the Chief to the lower level executives, it is distorted completely, so much so that **the original message is interpreted differently by each level in the organisation.**

The chief of the space center gets to know about the possibility of seeing Halley's Comet and decides that the entire organisation should witness this spectacle. He sends a memo to the Director.

Tomorrow evening at 20:00 hours, we will be able to see Halley's Comet in the sky through the naked eye. Since this is not an everyday event, everyone at the Center should assemble outside in their best clothes to watch it. If it rains, we will not be able to see it very well, in which case everyone should assemble in the Canteen.

To Director

By order of the Chief

The Director then sends the following memo to various Executive Directors.

By order of the Chief, we will be able to see "Halley's Comet" at 20:00 hours, tomorrow evening. If it is raining, we shall not be able to see it very well on site, in our best clothes. In that case, the disappearance of the Comet will be followed through in the Canteen. This is something which we cannot see happening every day.

Director

To,
Executive Directors

The Executive Director sends out memos to the Heads of Departments

By order of the Chief, we shall follow through, in our best clothes, the disappearance of the comet in the Canteen at 20:00 hrs, tomorrow evening. The Chief will tell us whether it is going to rain. This is something which we cannot see happening every day.

Executive Director

To,
Heads of Departments

The Heads of Departments send this message to their Managers -

If it is raining in the Canteen tomorrow evening, which is something we cannot see happening every day, our Chief in his best clothes will disappear at 20:00 hrs.   Head of Department To, All Managers,

Finally, each Manager sends the following notice to their Executives -

Tomorrow evening, at 20:00 hrs our Chief will disappear. It is a pity that we cannot see his happening every day.

Another type of organisational barrier is a **departmental barrier.** This means that **each department in an organisation functions in isolation** and there is no co-ordination or communication between them.

4. Channel Barriers: Wrong Choice of Channel is one of the main barriers to communication. Using a wrong medium of advertising, or conveying a message orally when a written letter would be more appropriate, are examples. The written channel is more appropriate when the communication is more formal or for keeping things on record, while emotional messages such as feelings about co-workers are better conveyed orally.

5. Linguistic and Cultural Barriers: When the **sender of the message uses a language that the receiver does not understand,** the communication will not succeed. Either the sender may be using a different or foreign language, or the language used may be too highly technical for the receiver to understand.

Linguistic barriers may also occur in cross-cultural advertising and distort the communication, when translating campaigns or slogans literally from one language to another. For example, Pepsi's slogan "Come Alive with Pepsi", when translated into Chinese, read "Pepsi brings your ancestors back from the grave!"

Cultural differences refer to **differences in values and perceptions, which may affect the interpretation of the message by the receiver.** For example, a joke about women may be taken in the wrong sense if the receiver belongs to a culture where women are highly respected.

6. Semantic Barriers: The word "semantics" refers to the meaning of words and the way in which they are used. For example, different words may have different meanings in different cultures. Failure to take this into consideration could lead to serious blunders.

Examples: Saying "The new product launch went like a bomb" in British English would mean that the new product launch was a success.

On the other hand, saying "The new product launch bombed" in American English would mean that the new Product was a disaster.

7. Non-verbal Barriers: This refers to the non-verbal communication that goes with a particular message. Non verbal communication includes the tone of voice, body language such as gestures and facial expressions, etc. **If the tone of the voice and body language are negative, the communication will fail,** however positive the spoken and written message is.

For example, if you happen to meet a long lost friend and say "I am delighted to meet you", but in a sad tone of voice, the exact opposite message will be conveyed!

Therefore, it is important to avoid giving conflicting signals, through the use of non-verbal communication.

1.10 Overcoming the Barriers to Communication

Certain steps can be taken, both at the organisational level as well as at the individual level, to effectively deal with the barriers to communication, in order to try to minimise them, if not eliminate them entirely –

Organisational Action

1. **Encourage Feedback:** Organisations should try to improve the communication system by getting feedback from the messages already sent. Feedback can tell the managers whether the message has reached the receiver in the intended way or not.

2. **Create a Climate of Openness:** A climate of trust and openness can go a long way in removing organisational barriers to communication. All subordinates or junior employees should be allowed to air their opinions and differences without fear of being penalised.

3. **Use Multiple Channels of Communication:** Organisations should encourage the use of multiple channels of communication, in order to make sure that the message reaches the intended receivers without fail. This means using a combination of both oral and written channels, as well as formal (official) and informal (unofficial) channels of communication.

Individual Action

1. **Active Listening:** This means **listening to the meaning of the speaker's words,** rather than **listening without hearing,** or **"passive listening".** Passive listening is a barrier to communication, whereas real communication takes place when we listen actively, with understanding. Listening is a skill which can be developed through proper training.

2. **Careful wording of messages:** Messages should be worded clearly and without ambiguity, to make sure that the message that is received is the same as the message is sent.

3. **Selection of Appropriate Channels:** Individuals should be competent enough to choose the right communication channel, depending on the situation.

Points to Remember

- Communication is a process involving the sorting, selecting and sending of symbols in such a way as to help the listener perceive and recreate in his own mind the meaning contained in the mind of the communicator.
- **Simon:** *"The question to be asked of any administrative process is: How does it influence the decisions of the individuals without communication, the answer must always be: It does not influence them at all."*
- **Features of Communication:**
  1. It is unavoidable.
  2. It is a two way exchange of information.
  3. It is a process.
  4. It involves a Sender and a Receiver of Information.
  5. It could be Verbal or Non-verbal.
  6. It is successful when the Receiver interprets the meaning in the same way as that intended by the Sender.
- **Elements of Communication:**
  1. Source
  2. Encoding
  3. Channel
  4. Receiver
  5. Decoding
  6. Feedback
- Communication is a *two – way process and a cyclic process.*
- **Principles of Communication-**
  1. Clarity
  2. Information
  3. Completeness
  4. Emphasis on attention
  5. Consistency
  6. Integration
  7. Use of Informal Organisation
  8. Two way communication
  9. To know the receiver
  10. Time
  11. Simplicity
  12. Communication network
  13. Use of media
  14. Feedback

- **Effective communication serves the following specific purposes in an organisation:**
  1. Greater Awareness of Organisational Goals and Teamwork
  2. Better Employer-employee Relationships
  3. Problem Solving
  4. Improved Performance
  5. Stronger Link between Manager and the External Environment
- **Barriers to Communication**
  1. Environmental barriers
  2. Individual barriers
  3. Organisational barriers
  4. Channel barriers
  5. Language and Cultural Barriers
  6. Semantic barriers
  7. Non-verbal Barrier
- **Overcoming barriers of communication:**
  Organisational Action
  1. Ecourage Feedback
  2. Create a climate of openness
  3. Use multiple channels of communication

  Individual Action
  1. Active Listening
  2. Careful wording of messages
  3. Selection of appropriate channels

FREQUENTLY ASKED QUESTIONS FROM UNIVERSITY OF PUNE EXAMINATIONS

1. Explain the process of communication. **[April 2007, 2008, 2009]**
2. Explain barriers and importance of communication. **[April 2007]**
3. Explain the scope of communication. **[Oct. 2007]**
4. Explain in detail principles of communication **[April 2009]**
5. State barriers in Communication. **[April 2009]**
6. What do you mean by Communication? Explains the barriers of Communication. **[April 2010]**
7. Define the term Communication. Explain the importance and principles of effective communication. **[Oct. 2010, April 2011]**
8. What is Communication? Explain in detail barriers of Communication. **[April 2011]**

Chapter ...2

METHODS AND CHANNELS OF COMMUNICATION

Contents ...

1.1 Introduction
1.2 Methods of Communication
1.3 Various Channels of Communication
    1.3.1 Vertical Communication
    1.3.2 Horizontal Communication
    1.3.3 Diagonal Communication
    1.3.4 Informal Communication
- Points to Remember
- Frequently Asked Questions from University of Pune Examination.

Learning Objectives ...

- To study the various methods of communication
- To study the channels of communication such as vertical, horizontal, diagonal and informal communication

1.1 Introduction

These days communication is possible through a vast variety of media. The Managing Director eager of communicating with the sales manager can summon him to his room, talk to him over the telephone, or send him a memo. If he wants to consult all the departmental heads, he would most probably convene a meeting. If information is to be transmitted to all the employees, a notice may be put on the notice board or a peon may circulate it among them, a senior officer may announce it over the public address system, or it may be printed in the office bulletin. Posters may be used to issue warnings. Communication with the Government departments and other agencies is generally conducted through written letters. General public can be reached through advertisements on the radio, television, theatre halls, or in the newspapers and popular journals. For communication to be effective, the communicator has to be very careful and judicious in the choice of media. This will depend on various factors like the urgency of the message, the time available, the expenditure involved and the intellectual and emotional level of the receivers. All the media available can be broadly classified into five groups:

(i) Written communication
(ii) Oral Communication
(iii) Visual Communication
(iv) Audio – visual communication; and
(v) Computer-based communication

1. **Written communication** includes letters, circulars, memos, telegrams, reports, minutes, forms and questionnaires, manuals etc. Everything that has been written and transmitted in the written form falls in the area of written communication.

2. **Oral Communication** includes face-to-face conversation, conversation over the telephone, radio broadcasts, interviews, group discussions, meetings, conferences and seminars, announcements over the public address system, speeches, etc.

3. **Visual Communication** includes gestures and facial expression. Organisations also make use of tables and charts, graphs, diagrams, posters, slides, film strips, etc as a means of visual communication.

4. **Audio-visual communication** encompasses television and films that make use of the visual impact along with narration.

5. **Computer-based communication** includes e-mail, voice mail, cellular phones, fax, etc.

Most often more than one medium may have to be simultaneously employed to make the communication effective. Face-to-face communication combines the oral form with the visual. Graphs and posters often combine the visual with the written form. A manager giving written instructions takes effort to explain them to a subordinate. In such a situation he simultaneously uses the oral and the written form of communication. A great deal can be communicated by the absence of communication, that is, by maintaining silence.

1.2 Methods of Communication

A message cannot be sent directly from the mind of the sender to the mind of the receiver. The message must be communicated either

- By use of words (i.e verbal communication), or
- By gestures, symbols or actions (i.e non-verbal communication)

Verbal and Non-verbal Communication

The following diagram explains these two categories of communication

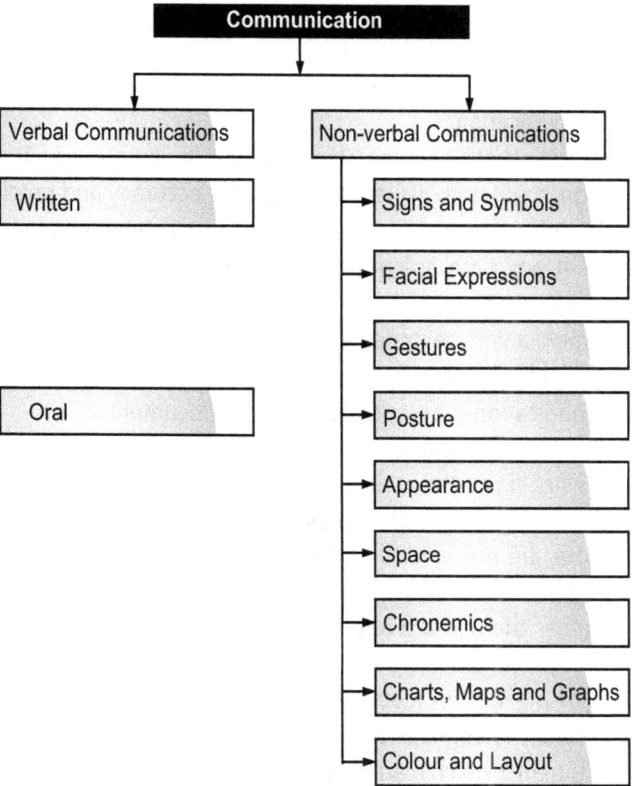

Fig. 2.1: Methods of Communication

Verbal Communication

Verbal communication consists of words of a language arranged in meaningful patterns. To convey a message through these words, they are arranged according to the rules of grammar so that they form a proper sequence. These messages may be shared in interpersonal (one to one), speaker – audience (one to many) and mass media (many to many) contexts. It should be effectively communicated so that the receiver perceives it, assigns it the right meaning and responds to it accordingly.

Verbal communication may be spoken (oral) or written. When effectively conveyed the spoken word will be listened to, and the written word will be read. Both oral and written communications are important in corporate communication and both have their benefits and drawbacks.

Written Communication

The purpose of written communication can be to provide a permanent record (archival), to notify someone (informative) or to get someone to do something (persuasive). When exchange of opinions is in a written form, rather than by spoken words, it is known as written communication. It includes letters, memos, reports, proposals, notices, minutes, circulars, manuals, newsletters and journals.

Though used less frequently than oral communication some of its advantages are:
1. Although it takes more time than oral communication, it is a planned and organised means of communication.
2. Written communication is usually formulated with great care. Therefore, in written communication, there is an insistence on greater accuracy and precision.
3. It can be referred to repeatedly. The receiver of a written communication can go over the message at any time again in the future. He can re-read till he thinks he has properly understood it.
4. Written communication becomes a permanent record of the organisation and can prove very useful for future reference.
5. Written communication is acceptable as a legal document.
6. Written documents are confidential.
7. The person who signs the written communication is answerable to any doubts regarding the document. It facilitates the process of assigning responsibilities. If communications are preserved in writing, it is much easier to assign responsibilities. In case a mistake is committed as a result of oral communication, it is very difficult to ascertain whether the mistake has been committed at the communicator's or at the receiver's end.
8. Many copies of the written matter can be photocopied or reprinted and distributed to a large number of people. In this way dissemination of information becomes easy.
9. Detailed documents which carry facts and statistics have to be maintained in a written format or else there is the possibility of deletion or skipping some important matter.

Despite being accurate and permanent; written communication has some limitations too.
1. One of the major limitations of written communication is that it is time-consuming. Accordingly the feedback also takes time.
2. Once it leaves the sender, he has no control over its progress. Only when he receives the response will he know the effect of his communication.
3. Expressions and feelings cannot be conveyed through written communication as effectively as oral communication.
4. Written communication is not accessible to those who are illiterate.
5. Good writing skills are necessary or else written communication will not convey the message as it is intended to be.
6. In case the receiver of a written communication has certain doubts or questions about the message, he cannot seek immediate clarification as is possible in oral messages.

Oral Communication

Oral communication includes face-to-face conversations, meetings, interviews, seminars, conferences, group discussions, telephonic conversations, teleconferencing, video conferencing and voice-mails. The contents could be formal or informal in nature. Oral communication is more often used because of the following reasons.

- Oral communication is quicker as many a times it is unplanned and spontaneous.
- The sender receives feedback almost immediately and can re-word or present his message in a better way. Immediate feedback helps the sender clarify any doubts the receiver would have.
- While reaching out to masses or groups of people oral communication is more useful, and more effective especially where illiterate masses are concerned.
- The modulation of the voice conveys the various moods of the speaker.
- The facial expressions speak much more than any languages. So speech is a better and more powerful method for persuasion and for convincing people.
- As it is not always as formal as written communication it helps to bond the sender and the receiver better. It is more personal.

Yet, oral communication is not without its limitations.

- As it is unplanned there are chances of mistakes or deletions in the messages.
- Retention of lengthy messages is difficult. When conveyed orally, important parts may be forgotten or missed.
- Recalling the whole message may not be possible.
- Oral communication has no permanent records (unless recorded on tape) and so has no legal validity. It cannot be referred to and has no accountability.
- If the receiver has not paid attention to what is being spoken, the sender may not get the required response. Sometimes, the sender may have to repeat the message (several times) for emphasis and clarity.
- Poor communicators may not be able to convey the message effectively.
- Oral communication may not be as confidential as written communication.

Non-Verbal Communication

This is a process of communication in which a person uses his expressions by way of signals in order to communicate his message. This does not require the use of words because a person can express his feelings through his body language. Under non-verbal communication, when one wants to show one's happiness, one smiles or gestures with one's hands or uses mild strokes on someone's back to show nearness and appreciation. Similarly, to show anger, one's face turns red and one faces difficulty in breathing. A person can communicate his feelings to others quickly and economically by using non-verbal form of communication. The receiver can easily understand what the sender is trying to say and what he is thinking about.

This communication is spontaneous and usually not deliberate or planned. There are many gestures, signs, symbols and signals that are accepted and understood universally. There are also many more non-verbal expressions that are specific to persons, regions, religions, cultures, countries and so on.

Inspite of its variety and complexity people rely more on nonverbal cues than their verbal counterparts, especially when one contradicts the other. For e.g you compliment your mother on the new dish she prepared but eat only half of what is served. Your verbal 'very tasty' does not match your action of not eating it. Words are relatively easier to control than natural gestures and expressions. A keen observer will be able to interpret the underlying meaning or intention of a non-verbal message and respond accordingly.

Though vast, the various forms of non-verbal communication have been grouped under different categories like body language, proxemics, signs and symbols, colours, time, spatial arrangements, maps and graphs, etc.

1. **Signs and Symbols**

As mentioned before there are some non-verbal messages which are universally known and accepted. Signs and symbols belong to this category. Signs stand for a particular message or they indicate a specific idea. On the roads we have 🅿 or 🚫 the first proxemics, parking allowed, and the second indicates 'parking not allowed'. Along the expressway we see 🍽 or ⛽ or 📞 which indicate that food, petrol or telephone facilities are available ahead. These signs are 'readable' by people all over the world. Blinking lights, traffic lights and sirens etc. are called signals. Signals are signs in motion.

Symbols are indicators or marks used as a standard representation of something. We have basic mathematical symbols +, -, x and ÷ language symbols (A, P, X, M,) musical notes (♪♩) chemical symbols [Fe (iron), Mn (managanese)] and so on. They have been developed by man to represent an idea. Besides these flags, coins, logos of the organisations etc. are also symbols. The moment people see the symbol ॐ in India we recognise it as 'Om' a Hindu symbol and the world sees it as a symbol related to India. So signs and symbols may be thought of as convenient modes of non-verbal communication.

2. **Body Language**

Unconsciously our body sends out many messages through the way we look at someone or something, we carry ourselves, we interact with others and the way we dress. Keen observers of these messages we will be able to collect much information other than what we contribute verbally. Body language will include the communication conveyed by the face (expressions), gestures, posture and even dress or appearance. They study of body movements is called *Kinesics*.

(a) **Facial Expressions:** The different parts of the face express several emotions and of these the eyes are the most expressive. Looking directly at someone shows boldness or arrogance, downcast eyes could indicate diffidence, shyness, fear or discomfort, averting your gaze could mean guilt and raising of eyebrows along with widening of the eye may suggest fear or surprise. The eyes, the eyebrows, the forehead and the mouth together could display many expressions.

Facial expression means the movement of the muscles of the face for showing emotions. Different emotions or feelings convey the emotional state of the individual.

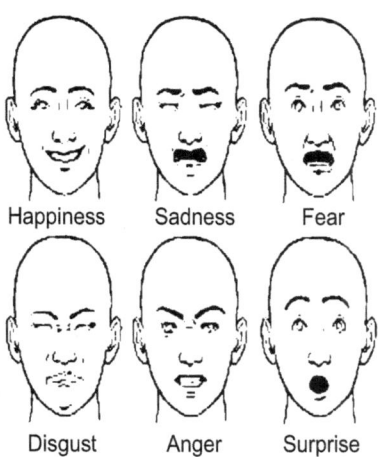

Facial Expression

(b) **Gestures:** The movements of the hands, arms, legs, head and shoulders are termed as gestures. A "Namaste", bending of the upper body (a bow), raising of the hand, a handshake are all various forms of greeting. When we require conveying a message to a person in a crowded room we mime the message using our own code. The way we place our palms, arms, hands, head, shoulders etc. while speaking, listening or reading, convey different meanings. Breaking knuckles, clenching fists, tilting of the head, slouching of shoulders, shaking of the head sideways or up and down all signify some meaning or the other. The same gesture could have different meaning in different contexts; and the same gesture with slight differences could send different messages. The raising of the hand to someone across the road is greeting, the same gesture at a meeting could mean 'I have something to say, may I? Or during an argument the same gesture could be a threat to say 'I'll hit you'. In a handshake the grip of the hands indicate much about the person to the other. A firm grip speaks of confidence, a limp grip – differences or disinterest, a fleeting touch – discomfort and so on. Gestures vary not only with context, but even with cultures.

Few examples

Waving Hands

Wagging the index finger to scold

Pointing index finger to accuse **Shrugging shoulders to show indifference**

(c) **Posture:** The way you sit, stand or walk, or the way you carry yourself speaks about your personality. Marching soldiers look smart, imagine them with hands in their pockets and swaggering along. As a child haven't you been told many times to stand erect, walk straight and sit properly? Here again the context decides the correct posture. At an official meeting the speaker should stand on both feet and be in command. The people listening should sit right - not stiff and upright throughout, nor slouched on the table either. Contestants at beauty pageants and models walking the ramp are trained to carry themselves well. Good posture conveys smartness and confidence.

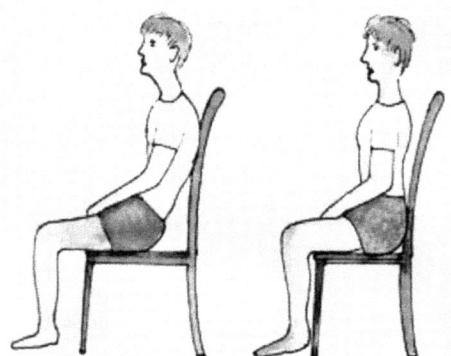

Posture

> **Body Postures show us that a person is**
> ❖ Confident, diffident, young, old, strong or weak
> ❖ Lazy (slouching posture)
> ❖ Overconfident (hands in the pocket posture)

(d) **Appearance:** Physical appearance may be difficult to alter. Although today cosmetic surgery and other 'corrective' measures can give you a new look. Here, by appearance we mean general grooming. We dress differently for different occasions. A wedding in the family, a visit next door, a friend's birthday party, attending an interview or going to college, calls for different dressing.

(e) **Space:** Proxemics is the study of space. Each person occupies space and considers the space around him as his space. He may allow some people to cross in to this space; some people are referred at the boundary and some others still further away. Your close family and friends may touch you or be in close contact while speaking. When you interact with colleagues or acquaintances you maintain some distance from them. This distance will depend on how close or comfortable you are with the person. Researchers have identified various zones as intimate space (close family and friends), personal space (for colleagues and friends), social space (acquaintances, superiors, subordinates) and formal or public space (meetings, gatherings). A person keeping to these specified distances may change with context and culture.

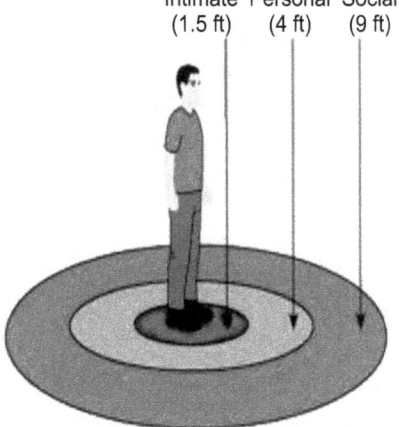

Space is the personal distance a person keeps (often unconsciously) with people, events and its surrounding.

- ❖ Actions like shaking hands, touching or whispering use intimate space.
- ❖ Interaction with good friends uses personal space
- ❖ Attending a marriage ceremony uses social space.
- ❖ Public gatherings use public space.

(e) **Chronemics**

Chronemics is the way people plan, execute and react to time and its effect on the interpretation of messages they send and receive. It refers to the element of time in communication. How does time factor affect communication? In fact, time is a powerful tool of non-verbal communication. Time perceptions can be shown through punctuality, willingness to wait, speed of speech, pause or even through the amount of time people are willing to listen to the other person. The time factor plays a vital role in non-verbal communication also.

The general understanding of Chronemics is useful in inter-cultural communication also. The perception and handling of time in communication may vary from culture to culture. Sometimes, while conversing, a person starts answering even before the speaker has finished the question. This may be considered as an insult in certain cultures, whereas in some other cultures, immediate response to the question may be expected.

3. Charts, Maps and Graphs

Verbal communication could be made more effective with some non-verbal inputs like sketches, charts, maps and graphs. A lecture on some geographical aspect could be more interesting when explained with the help of a map. An animal's circulatory function would be better understood if accompanied by a sketch or diagram. Sometimes these non-verbal supplements may be able to convey messages by itself. A pie-diagram with the right title and basic details can be self explanatory.

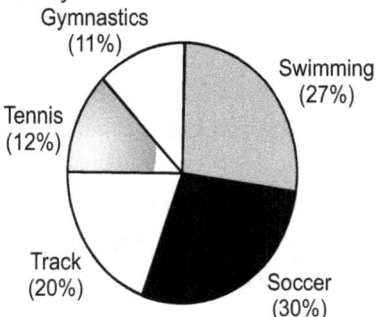

Participation of various sports in a sports competition

Charts, figures and tables often direct the audience to the central theme of the presentation. A well-planned chart, for example, can quickly summarise pages of text while emphasizing the most important points. Sketches help related topics, graphs supplement mathematical and statistical data, and maps make directions to places and environmental studies interesting and so on.

4. Colour and Layout

The use of colour is symbolic. Certain colours are associated with some political parties. In an international sports meet countries are identified by the colour of their jerseys. Some professionals have uniforms by which they are identified (doctors, air-hostesses, lawyers etc.) In India red is an auspicious colour, while black is inauspicious. Most Christian brides wear a white gown on their wedding day while in most Hindu weddings brides never wear white. So colours reflect different ideas depending on cultures and countries. Business houses have logos designed in specific colours so that they are identified by those. For example, The logo of McDonalds big yellow 'M' is easily identified.

Besides colours, the layout of a structure, the design of a room, the arrangement of furniture and the placing of doors, windows and artifacts are of great importance today. While constructing, builders and architects take care to follow Vaastu-shastra or Feng shui Rules to bring in positive energy to the building. We appreciate the ambience and décor of some houses, offices and hotels while we are uncomfortable in some others. This only proves that arrangement; design and colour speak much about than the premises.

1.3 Various Channels of Communication

In an organisation, information flows forward, backwards and sideways. This flow of information is called communication. Communication channels refer to the way this information flows within the organisation. There are many different types of communication channels available for managers to use. The types of communication channels are grouped into three main groups: formal, informal and unofficial.

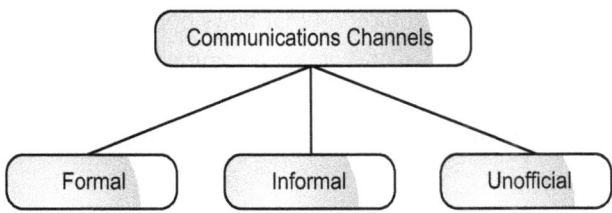

Fig. 2.2: Communication Channels

Formal communication flows along prescribed channels were all members desirous of communicating with one another are obliged to follow:
   A. Vertical Communication
      1. Upward Communication
      2. Downward Communication
   B. Horizontal communication
   C. Cross channel communication

Informal Communication is the transmission of information through nonofficial channels within the organisation.
   1. Grapevine

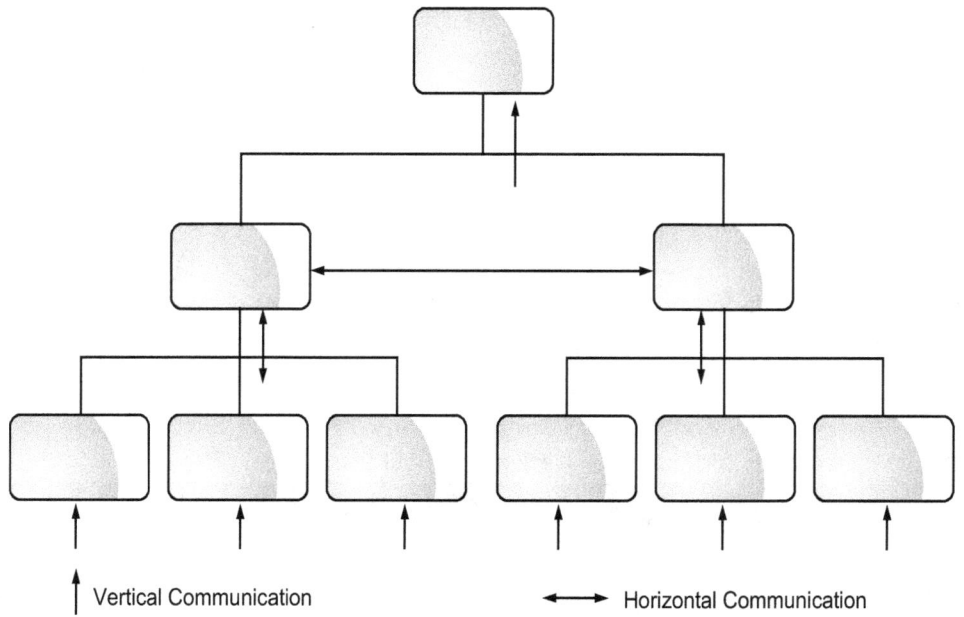

Fig. 2.3: Formal Communication

1.3.1 Vertical Communication

Vertical communication is communication that flows both up and down the organisation, usually along formal reporting lines-that is, it is the communication that takes place between managers and their superiors and subordinates. Vertical communication may involve only two persons, or it may flow through several different organisational levels.

Downward communication

Traditionally organisational communication meant only downward communication, as the belief was that the management commanded and the employees worked. Today, organisations have realised that they have to facilitate and encourage their personnel to willingly contribute and to learn, to be participative, responsible and accountable in their activities. For the success of an organisation all the people in it should change the way they think and operate.

Downward communication occurs when information flows down the hierarchy from superiors to subordinates. Examples include circulars, emails, memos, etc.

Objectives of Downward Communication

Communication from a superior to a subordinate may be about orders or instructions, guidance, advice or solving problems. The following are the objectives of downward communication:

- To give specific job instructions and directives.
- To inform about organisational rules and regulations.

- To apprise subordinates about their performance.
- To highlight the link between the job, the employee's performance and the organisation's success.
- To be supportive in their organisational and personal problems.

Downward communication may be conveyed by writing or speaking. Writing could be in the form of letters, notice, memos, circulars, bulletins, posters and even annual reports. Oral downward communication could be by issuing orders and instructions, informing, educating or training through meetings. Technology is frequently used for downward communication today. It is easy to telephone a subordinate and easier still to e-mail information to several subordinates at the same time.

Merits of Downward Communication

1. **Valuable for the organisation:** Downward communication is the most essential component of an organisation. The organisation uses downward communication to communicate essential official information to employees.
2. **Valuable for Employees:** Downward communication is valuable for employees as they are well informed about their work from time to time. It provides them motivation and enhances the morale of employees.
3. **Disciplined organisation:** Through downward communication, division of responsibility and accountability brings about discipline, satisfaction, harmony and co-operation among the employees.
4. **Involvement in Organisation:** In downward communication, the employees carry a feeling of participation in the management of the organisation. They regard themselves as an important part of the organisation.

Though downward communication flows from a higher authority to a lower one and is the earliest channel of organisational communication it has its drawbacks and limitations.

Some of the limitations are

(1) **One-way communication:** In several cases a superior still behaves in an authoritative manner and does not encourage feedback (upward communication). He may instruct but will not entertain clarifications. To avoid face-to-face interaction most of his communication may be in writing or through e-mails. The reasons could be that the superior is not sure of the information he is passing on or that he is diffident of facing subordinates. He may not want to be physically present because the information he is conveying is unpleasant or that he would like to be only heard not seen. Whatever the reasons, a superior has to be responsible and is accountable for his actions. So he has to ensure that he maintains adequate contact with his subordinates and encourages two-way communication.

(2) Difference in values and perceptions: It is common for the superior to be committed to the total organisation, while the subordinate relates to his department or sub-group alone. The superiors visualise their performance in terms of long-term goals while subordinates see theirs in terms of immediate outcomes. Superiors typically view their contributions in terms of achievement while subordinates are more likely to see themselves as only contributing long hours and hard work. Such dissimilar viewpoints can be barriers to downward communication because subordinates may filter out parts of the downward messages conveyed to them.

(3) Mistrust: The feeling of mistrust appears when there is lack of frequent superior – subordinate contact. The subordinate knows that the superior controls his rewards and each downward message is viewed with mistrust and some concealed motive. For e.g. when an employee receives a transfer order, he views it as a punishment. He feels that the superior needs to promote somebody else so he is being moved out to pave way for 'somebody'.

(4) Inner conflicts of Leadership: The pressures of their 'position' can cause inner conflicts or status anxiety in a superior. He is torn between the responsibilities of his 'status' and the desire to be popular among subordinates. In his attempt to be a 'responsible' superior, he may end up being under communicative. Decisions made without consulting departmental heads, information passed down withholding relevant background details and actions ordered before discussions with employees concerned could cause confusion in subordinate's mind. On the other hand, the desire to be liked by his subordinates could create the over communicative superior.

(5) Resistance to authority: An employee generally believes that all communication from a higher authority will be anti-employee and if at all there is a positive one, there would be an unpleasant motive for it. So any downward communication is viewed with hostility. They accept or acknowledge only parts of the message that they are comfortable with, ignoring the other parts.

Upward communication

Upward communication is the interpersonal process, which is a response to the downward flow of communication. Upward communication consists of messages from subordinates to superiors. Although it is the channel for communication from the subordinate to the superior for several other matters as well, it is predominantly considered to be only a feedback channel. One study has shown that employees felt that communication with superiors to be the most important and satisfying type of communication, yet the same study showed this communication to be the most difficult to perform. Upward communication can be effective only with the encouragement of the higher authority.

Objectives of Upward Communication

Just as downward communication has certain objectives to fulfill so does the upward communication. Subordinates need to inform superiors on various aspects of organisational development besides responding to downward communication. The objectives of upward communication are:

- To respond to downward communication like orders, directives and instructions.
- To inform about commencement and progress of departmental activities.
- To suggest and submit ideas for organisational development.
- To encourage participation of subordinates in the decision making process.
- To improve inter personal relationships.

Upward communication will depend on downward communication. The response to orders and instructions will be positive only if they have been conveyed clearly. Subordinates can improve their performance if they are guided and helped to overcome their weaknesses periodically. Inculcating in them a sense of belonging to the organsiation makes them more responsible. They must be encouraged to give suggestions especially on matters related to their work. It is the attitude of the superior towards his subordinate that will decide on the quality of upward communication in an organisation.

Merits of Upwards Communication

1. **Feedback:** Through upward communication the management receives requisite feedback. The management ensures whether the instructions given to the employees have been properly understood and followed. Upward communication helps the employees to express what they think of the organisation and its policies.
2. **Positive recommendations:** A positive suggestion given by the employees helps the organisation to grow. In turn, it promotes the welfare of the employees as well.
3. **Conducive and Healthy organisational environment:** Upward communication creates harmony and improves employer and employee relations in the benefit of the organisation.
4. **Channel for unexpressed emotions:** Upward communication provides an opportunity to the employees to express their grievances. The management has to consider the employees problem for smooth functioning of the organisation. The authentic and critical grievances are redressed because of upward communication

It has been found that the flow of upward communication has several barriers. It is possible to overcome these limitations if the management provides employees the right environment for communication.

Some of the limitations are

(1) **Attitude of the Subordinate:** There is always a tendency on the part of the subordinates to transmit those messages upwards, that they feel will improve their standing with their bosses and to withhold information that will damage their image.

Thus, there is deliberate distortion of information. Stronger the interest in advancement or promotion, greater is the chance for distortion. Subordinates are also reluctant to be bearers of unfavourable information, as they fear it will reflect negatively on them and their performance.

(2) **Attitude of the Superior**: Superiors are also responsible for this distortion of upward communication. They maintain threatening, mistrustful and distant relationships with their subordinates. They do not encourage subordinates who are willing to face them with challenging or unpleasant information. They perceive such subordinates as 'troublemakers'.

(3) **Organisational structure:** Some organisations follow rigid structures and procedures. They could block upward communication. The physical distance between superiors and subordinates also restrict upward communication. In some larger organisations the senior executives could be functioning at the corporate/ divisional headquarters while workers are in field offices or retail outlets. On the other hand, within the same office, superiors remain inaccessible to subordinates. There may be some subordinates who decide what information should reach these superiors. They ensure that only pleasant messages reach the superiors.

(4) **Skipping ranks:** Subordinates find it convenient to relate to superiors who are friendly. They ignore their superior and approach the more senior person who may be friendly but is not their boss. For e.g. a junior executive who is not friendly with the officer above him approaches the senior manager with a request. If the senior manager accedes to the request there are bound to be breaks in the communication channels – between the officer and the junior executive and between the officer and the senior manager.

1.3.2 Horizontal Communication

Communication with persons of relatively equal status in an organisation is termed as horizontal or lateral communication. Horizontal communication ensures coordinated cross-functional efforts in achieving organisational goals. Communication with peers provides the much required social support for a person. They tend to turn towards their peers for support than to those above and below them. This may work well or adversely for an organisation.

Objectives of Horizontal Communication

Studies have shown that in organisations, horizontal communication takes up more time than vertical communication. Personnel who occupy almost equal status and handle similar responsibilities will have much to share and learn. Some of the objectives of horizontal communication are:

1. To coordinate functions throughout the organisation.
2. To share information.
3. To solve problems.
4. To resolve conflicts.

For coordination of activities, information has to be shared. Data collected by one department could be useful for the functioning of another department. Problems affecting the departments could be solved by employing brainstorming sessions. Such interactive sessions could bring out valuable ideas. Conflicts between individuals or departments could be resolved if the two parties concerned or their departmental representatives meet, discuss and find amicable solutions. Sometimes horizontal communication serves as a substitute for vertical communication when it encourages subordinates to resolve conflicts and to take decisions without the aid of their superiors.

Merits of Horizontal Communication

1. **Efficiency:** Horizontal channel of communication improves efficiency and saves time. Spontaneous and prompt decision making helps in critical situations of the organisation.
2. **Increases Productivity:** Productivity and efficiency of the employee's increases due to horizontal channel of communication.
3. **Limits informal communication:** Horizontal channel brings employees closer. It enables them to discuss matters directly and personally. This controls the growth of rumours within the organisation.
4. **Better Co-ordination:** Horizontal channel of communication promotes better co-ordination and in turn increases co-operation among the employees.

Though written communication in the form of reports, letters or memos are used for horizontal communication, oral communication is more common. Face-to-face interactions and meetings being the most frequently used oral communication.

Some of the limitations of horizontal communication are

(1) **Increased specialisation:** We live in a world of specialisation. For e.g. Even within a department, two people occupying similar status may be in-charge of two different projects or areas, so their common interests may be few. This affects communication between them. Then the lack of communication between personnel of two departments can be easily visualised. The larger the organisation the more the variety of jobs to be handled and so more the specialisation.

(2) **Lack of recognition and reward:** Though horizontal communication is a vibrant channel of communication there is not much encouragement from the organisation.

(3) **Suppression of differences:** Some people are too diplomatic and will not express disagreement. They would prefer to go with the group rather than speak up or question.

(4) **Ego clashes:** As horizontal communication is between peers, ego clashes are very common. Unhealthy competition, projecting oneself better than one's peers, withholding information, so that it hampers the work of another are some of the petty tactics pursued by people of same status. Only mature behaviour and giving importance to organisational goals can overcome this barrier.

1.3.3 Diagonal Communication

Diagonal Communication is the communication that takes place between people of similar status but of different organisations. When the CEO of a company communicates with the CEO of another company it is diagonal communication. When a teacher communicates with a parent of a PTA meeting, it is diagonal communication. Face to face and written communication are the means employed, and the communication is between people of equal status.

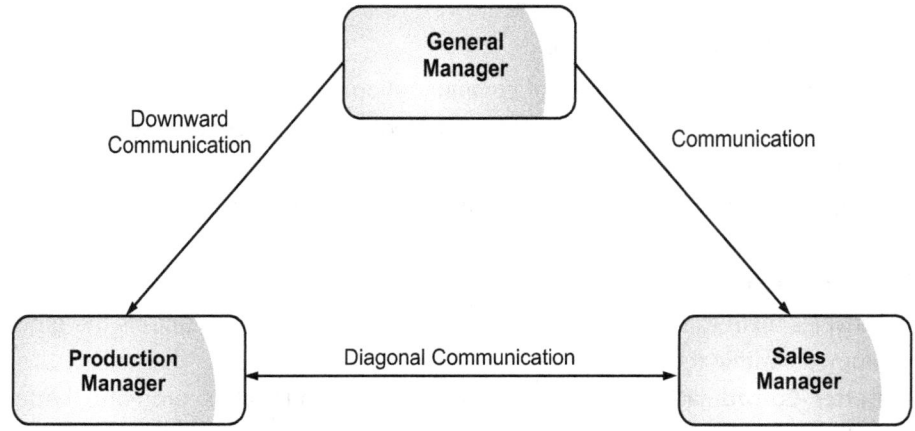

Fig. 2.4: Diagonal Communication

Merits of Diagonal Communication

1. **Commitment towards organisation:** Diagonal communication provides opportunities to the employees to interact with the managers of the other organisation, which in turn increases the confidence of the employees and ultimately enhances the commitment of the employees towards the organisation.
2. **Improves Coordination:** Diagonal communication improves coordination through information meetings, formal conferences, lunch hour meetings, etc.

Limitations of Diagonal Communication

1. **Encroachment:** As diagonal communication promotes interaction of employees of different organisation, it brings about a feeling of encroachment in the minds of the Superior and they feel as if they are avoided and overthrown by the subordinate, which becomes a serious limitation of the diagonal communication.
2. **Reluctant for executing suggestions:** As the superiors feel that they are avoided and not solicited by the subordinate, they may be reluctant to execute the suggestions and recommendations given by the subordinates.
3. **Chaos:** The non acceptance and non execution of suggestions and recommendations of the subordinates leads to chaos and disorder in the organisation.

1.3.4 Informal Communication

Grapevine

Informal communication, also known as the grapevine, is not a planned or deliberately created channel of communication. It is free from all formalities. No formal organisational chart is followed to convey messages. It is based on the informal relations of the two persons, the sender and the receiver of communication. It runs in all directions – horizontal, vertical, diagonal. A general manager may develop contacts with a worker at the lowest level and communicate certain important information relating to him direct to the worker. It is an example of informal communication. It is the result of the natural desire of people to communicate with each other when they come into contact on a regular basis. When interaction takes place among them, a small social group emerges spontaneously, and members of the group develop their own communication system known as informal communication channel, or the grapevine. Most informal communication is oral, but widespread use of e-mail has made informal written communication more popular.

Types of Grapevine

1. **Single Strand Chain:** In this type of chain 'A' tells something to 'B' who tells it so 'C' and so on it goes down the line. This chain is the least accurate in passing on the information.

    Fig. 2.5: Single Strand

2. **Gossip Chain:** In this person speaks out and tells everyone the information he or she has obtained. This chain is often used when information or a message regarding an interesting but 'non-job-related' nature is being conveyed.

    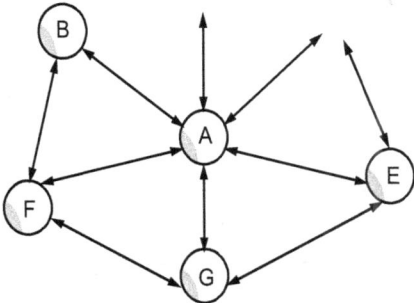

    Fig. 2.6: Gossip Chain

3. **Cluster Chain:** In this type of chain 'A' tells something to a few selected individuals and others also relay the information selectively.

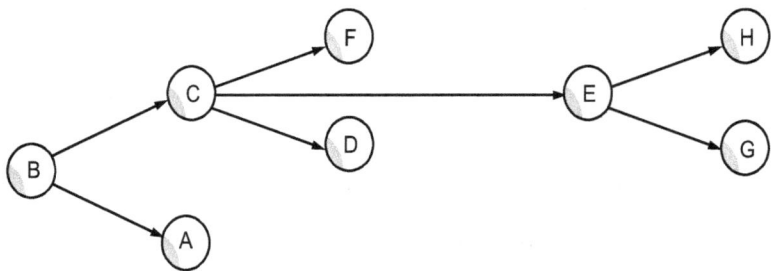

Fig. 2.7: Cluster Chain

4. **Probability Chain:** In this type of chain individuals are indifferent to, or not really interested in the persons to whom they are passing some information. They just tell at random, and those people in turn tell others at random. This chain is found when the information is somewhat interesting but not really significant.

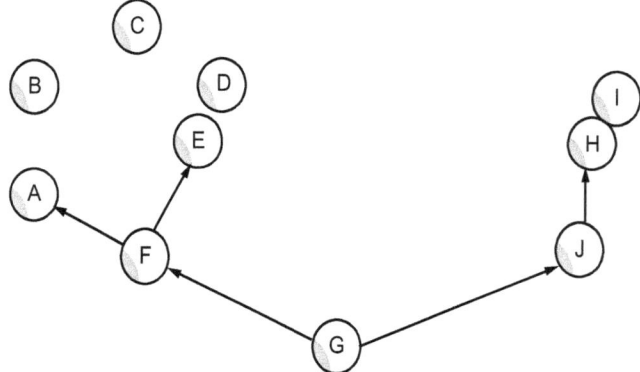

Fig. 2.8: Probability chain

Merits of Grapevine

1. **Quick diffusion of information:** The speed with which information is transmitted through the grapevine is remarkable. Rumours, they say, spread like wild fire. Just spot a leader of the grapevine and give him some information, cleverly describing it as 'top secret', and within minutes, it will have reached everybody.
2. **Organisational unity and Cohesion:** The existence of the grapevine proves that the workers are interested in their associates. The very fact that they talk among themselves helps to promote organisational solidarity and cohesion, properly used, the grapevine may even raise the morale of the workers.
3. **Safety control device:** Apprehensions experienced by workers on matters like promotions and retrenchments become an obsession with them. Talking about them may not alleviate their fears, but it certainly provides them emotional relief. Thus, the grapevine acts as a kind of safety-control device for the unexpressed emotions of the subordinates.

4. **Feedback:** The grapevine provides feedback to the management. It enables them to know what the subordinates think about the organisation and its various activities.
5. **Addition to other Channels:** All information cannot be transmitted to the employees through the official channels. If there is some useful information unsuitable for being transmitted through official channels, it can be transmitted through the grapevine.

Limitations of Grapevine

1. **Misrepresentation:** The grapevine respects nobody and it may ascribe the worst possible motives to the noblest of people. Thus, one of the major drawbacks of the grapevine is that it may spread baseless or distorted news which may sometimes prove harmful even to the employees.
2. **Incomplete information:** The grapevine information is usually incomplete. So it may be misunderstood or misinterpreted.
3. **Detrimental pace:** The pace with which the grapevine transmits information may even be damaging. A rumour may have spread and caused serious damaged before the management becomes aware of it and can take any rectifying step.
4. **Loss of Confidentiality:** Confidential information often leaks out through informal communication. Thus, the network of informal communication can be used by management only with due safety measure.
5. **Lack of Authenticity:** Informal communication spreads by word – of –mouth. It may not be supported by tangible facts. This would make the grapevine information unbelievable.
6. **Problem in Fixing Responsibility:** Origin of information flow cannot be ascertained in this channel. It is, therefore, difficult to hold anybody responsible for spreading false information.

Points to Remember

- Means of communication can be broadly classified into five groups:
  (i) Written communication
  (ii) Oral Communication
  (iii) Visual Communication
  (iv) Audio – visual communication and
  (v) Computer-based communication
  - Verbal communication consists of words of a language arranged in meaningful patterns.
  - Non Verbal - The purpose of written communication could be to provide a permanent record (archival), to notify someone (informative) or to get someone to do something (persuasive).

- There are some non-verbal messages which are universally known and accepted. Signs and symbols belong to this category.
- Body language includes commmunication conveyed by face (expressions), gestures, posture and appearance. The study of body movements is called *Kinesics*.
- Body Language includes Facial Expressions, Gestures, Posture, Appearance, Space and Chronemics
- The types of communication channels are grouped into three main groups: formal, informal and unofficial.
  - Vertical communication is communication that flows both up and down the organisation, usually along formal reporting lines-that is, it is the communication that takes place between managers and their superiors and subordinates.
  - Downward communication occurs when information flows down the hierarchy from superiors to subordinates
- The objective of downward communication is to give specific directions to subordinates about the job entrusted and to explain organisational policies and procedures.
- Limitations of Downward Communication include under communication, over communication, delay, loss of information and distortion of message
- Upward communication consists of messages from subordinates to superiors.
- The objectives of upward communication are:
  - To respond to downward communication like orders, directives and instructions.
  - To inform about commencement and progress of departmental activities.
  - To suggest and submit ideas for organisational development.
  - To encourage participation of subordinates in the decision making process.
  - To improve inter personal relationships.
- Advantages of Upward Communication
  1. Feedback
  2. Positive recommendation
  3. Conducive and Healthy organisation environment
- Limitations of Upward Communication
  1. Attitude of subordinate
  2. Attitude of superior
  3. Organisational structure
  4. Skipping ranks
- Communication with persons of relatively equal status in an organisation is termed as horizontal or lateral communication.

- The objectives of horizontal communication are:
  1. To coordinate functions throughout the organisation.
  2. To share information.
  3. To solve problems.
  4. To resolve conflicts.
- Advantages of Horizontal Communication
  1. Efficiency
  2. Increase Productivity
  3. Limits informal communication
  4. Better Co-ordination
- Limitations of Horizontal Communication are
  1. Increased specialisation
  2. Lack of recognition and reward
  3. Suppression of differences
  4. Ego clashes
- Diagonal Communication is the communication that takes place between people of similar status but of different organisations.
- Advantages of Diagonal communication are
  1. Commitment towards organisations
  2. Improves coordination
- Limitations of Diagonal Communication are
  1. Encroachment
  2. Reluctant for executing suggestions
  3. Chaos
- Informal communication, also known as the grapevine, is not a planned or deliberately created channel of communication. It is free from all formalities.
- It is based on the informal relations of the two persons, the sender and the receiver of communication. It runs in all directions – horizontal, vertical, diagonal.
- Types of Grapevine
  1. Single strand chain
  2. Gossip chain
  3. Cluster chain
  4. Probability chain
- Advantages of Grapevine
  1. Quick diffusion of information
  2. Organisational unity and cohesion
  3. Safety control device
  4. Feedback
  5. Addition to other channels

- Limitations of Grapevine
    1. Misrepresentation
    2. Incomplete information
    3. Detrimental pace
    4. Loss of confidentiality
    5. Lack of authenticity
    6. Problem in fixing responsibility

FREQUENTLY ASKED QUESTIONS FROM UNIVERSITY OF PUNE EXAMINATIONS

1. State the advantages of written Communication **[April 2006, 2008]**
2. State the disadvantages of oral Communication **[April 2007]**
3. Explain the advantages of Written communication **[Oct.2010]**
4. Describe the various methods of Communication **[April 2011]**
5. Distinguish between oral communication and written Communication. **[April 2012]**

Chapter ...3

SOFT SKILLS

Contents ...
- 3.1 Soft Skills
    - 3.1.1 Introduction
    - 3.1.2 Meaning
    - 3.1.3 Definition
    - 3.1.4 Importance of Soft Skill
- 3.2 Elements of Soft Skill
    - 3.2.1 Grooming Manners and Etiquettes
    - 3.2.2 Effective Speaking
    - 3.2.3 Interview Skills
    - 3.2.4 Listening Skills
    - 3.2.5 Group Discussion
    - 3.2.6 Oral Presentation
- Points to Remember
- Frequently Asked Questions from University of Pune Examination

Learning Objectives ...
- To learn about the definition and importance of soft skills
- To learn the elements of soft skill – including the grooming manners, effective speaking, interview skills, listening skills, group discussion and oral presentation

3.1 Soft Skills

3.1.1 Introduction

'Soft skills' is a sociological term which refers to the cluster of personality traits, social graces, ability with language, personal habits etc. In other words, a set of skills that influence how we interact with each other are known as 'Soft Skills'. It includes abilities such as effective communication, creativity, analytical thinking, diplomacy, flexibility, change-readiness and problem solving, leadership, team building and speaking and listening skills. Personal management skills such as attitudes and behaviours that drive ones potential for growth and teamwork skills are also comprised in soft skills.

3.1.2 Meaning

Soft skills include all facets of general skills that cover the intellectual aspect and non-academic skills of an individual. These skills help an individual in developing better interaction, performance and career prospects in an organisation.

3.1.3 Definitions

1. *"Soft skills are personal management skills such as attitudes and behaviour that drives ones potential for growth and team work skills".*
2. *"Soft skills are the kind of skills needed to perform jobs where job requirements are defined in terms of expected outcomes."*
3. *"Soft skill is a set of skill that influences how we interact with each other. It includes such abilities as effective communication, creativity, analytical thinking, diplomacy, flexibility, change-readiness and problem solving, leadership, team building and listening skills."*

3.1.4 Importance of Soft Skills

1. **Improves communication skills:** Communication is a medium to express ones thoughts, ideas, feelings, emotions, etc. The ability to communicate is highly essentially at every work place. Communication skill can be made more effective with the aid of developing soft skill in an individual. With the help of soft skills, an individual can deliver his idea clearly and confidently either orally or in writing. It also enhances usage of technology during presentations. Soft skills facilitate people from varied background to communicate in an effective way.

2. **Develops overall personality:** Soft skill is an aid to develop an overall personality of an individual in order to facilitate him for delivering his best performance at the work place. It also inculcates positive approach towards work among employees. It boosts the morale of the employees and makes them understand the need of the organisation professionally in terms of economic crisis, environmental, social and cultural aspects.

3. **Team Building:** Every individual working in an organisation is unique. Some employees may be comfortable working within a group, while others may prefer to work alone. Soft skill helps an individual to overcome these differences and build a good rapport and work effectively with others as a team. Moreover, it improves the ability of an individual to recognise and respect other's attitude, behaviour and beliefs.

4. **Problem solving ability:** Soft skill enhances an individual's ability to identify and analyse problems in critical situations and to come up with acceptable appraisal for the given problem. In addition to these, Soft skill develops an aptitude among

individuals to find novel ideas and look for alternative feasible solution. It helps to assimilate and accommodate oneself to the diverse working environment.
5. **Customer service skills:** Customer service skill is one of the most essential skills an entrepreneur or business owner looks for while hiring important folks who will take care of their customer. Today's world is more customer centric which demands from an organisation to deliver customised services as per their expectations. In turn, to meet these expectations of their customers, the organisation concentrates on training their employees to improve their customer service skills such as developing patience, attentiveness, clear communication skills, knowledge of the product, time management skills, persuasion skills, willingness to learn, etc.
6. **Entrepreneurship skills:** Soft skills play an important role in the development of the employees as well as for the entrepreneur. Entrepreneur is the person who binds the employees with the organisation for the achievement of organisational goals. The entrepreneur should possess the soft skill of identifying, exploring, exploiting and building business opportunities and remain competitive in the critical business environment. Thus, soft skills are equally important for the entrepreneur to possess.
7. **Leadership skills:** The ability to lead effectively is based on a number of key skills. These skills are highly sought after by the employers as they involve dealing with people in such a way as to motivate, enthuse and build respect. Soft skill enables an individual to understand and take turn as a leader and provides him with capability to lead and supervise a team.

3.2 Elements of Soft skill
3.2.1 Grooming Manners

Grooming is the process of making yourself attractive and presentable. In simple words grooming means the things which you do to make yourself and your appearance tidy and pleasant. Personal Grooming is the term for how people take care of their body and appearance. Habits that are considered in personal grooming include dressing, make up, taking care of one's teeth and skin, etc. Appearance, clothes and manners do not make the man; but, when he is made, they greatly improve his appearance whether this is real or imaginary; the most important fact is that your appearance influences the opinions of everyone around you. Your professionalism, intelligence and the trust people form in you depends on your appearance.

Importance of Grooming
- In the business atmosphere it is extremely important to have knowledge of grooming skills because you deal with people of different cultures on a regular basis and should always aim to make the best first impressions, lasting impressions or you risk losing potential opportunities for yourself.

- A person with bad personal grooming habits can be spotted from anywhere. Therefore, personal grooming is highly essential.
- A clean and neat appearance inspires confidence. Grooming is important if you want to feel confident and project a positive self-image of yourself. For a good impression, grooming is must.
- Grooming is an external appearance, which is the window of your personality to the world. External appearance is very important as it portray the first impression to others about your personality.

What is Etiquette?

Business etiquette is a set of rules that govern the way people interact with one another in business, with customers, suppliers, with inside or outside bodies. It is all about conveying the right image and behaving in an appropriate way. Etiquette refers to behaving in a socially responsible way.

Etiquette refers to guidelines which control the way a responsible individual should behave in the society

Need for Etiquette

- Etiquette makes you a cultured individual who leaves his mark wherever he goes.
- Etiquette teaches you the way to talk, walk and most importantly behave in the society.
- Etiquette is essential for an everlasting first impression. The way you interact with your superiors, parents, fellow workers, friends speak a lot about your personality and up-bringing.
- Etiquette enables the individuals to earn respect and appreciation in the society. No one would feel like talking to a person who does not know how to speak or behave in the society. Etiquette inculcates a feeling of trust and loyalty in the individuals. One becomes more responsible and mature. Etiquette helps individuals to value relationships.

Types of Etiquette

1. **Social Etiquette:** Social etiquette is important for an individual as it teaches him how to behave in the society.
2. **Corporate Etiquette:** Corporate etiquette refers to how an employee should behave while he is at work. Each one needs to maintain the dignity and the decorum of the organisation.
3. **Meeting Etiquette:** Meeting etiquette refers to a manner one need to adopt when he is attending any meeting, seminar, presentation and so on. Listen to what the other person has to say. Never enter a meeting room without a notepad and pen. It is important to jot down important points for future reference.
4. **Telephone Etiquette:** It is essential to learn how one should interact with the other person over the phone. Telephone etiquette refers to the way an individual should speak on the phone. Never put the other person on long holds. Make sure you greet the other person. Take care of your pitch and tone.

5. **Business Etiquette:** Business etiquette includes ways to conduct a certain business. Don't ever cheat customers. It is simply unethical.

Some basic etiquettes to be followed in Business Dealings

1. **Introduction:** Always introduce your staff to others whenever the opportunity arises, unless you know that they are already acquainted. It makes people feel appreciated, regardless of their rank or position.
2. **Being polite:** Being polite is the basic form of courtesy highly essential in a casual professional atmosphere. It is always nice to send a handwritten thank you note as it gives an emotional touch rather than a formal email conveying thank you.
3. **Not to be over aggressive:** People by nature are always eager to offer their opinions or often interrupt others when they speak. It is rude and shows disregard for the opinions of others. Remember, be assertive, not aggressive.
4. **Proper language:** In business dealings, always one should be careful to choose words wisely. Rude, offensive or slang language is undesirable.
5. **Don't chitchat:** Gossiping at business place can lead to adverse problems for self and others. Gossips are harmful for the organisation. One should try to avoid talking about someone who is not present.
6. **Don't spy:** Everyone is entitled to private conversations, in person or over the phone. The same goes for e-mail; don't stand over someone's shoulder and read their e-mails.
7. **Recognise others:** At the workplace when an employee approaches you, acknowledge him or her. If you are in the middle of some important work, it is all right to ask them to wait a minute while you finish your work. Being busy is not an excuse to ignore others.
8. **Punctual:** Being punctual shows others that you value their time. One should always try to avoid getting late for the work entrusted to them. Punctuality creates disciplines in the organisation.
9. **Avoid phone calls in Meetings:** When you are in a meeting, do not attend a phone call, which distracts your focus on the meeting. It also makes meetings last longer because the partaker of the meeting keep losing focus.
10. **Paying attention when others speak:** Effort should be made to truly listen to what others say. One should put an effort and patiently wait for the other person to finish their talk and then one can move on to the next thing. Take the time to respond to others queries and show an interest in the other person's thoughts.

3.2.2 Effective Speaking

Good public speaking is simply the art of good conversation carried a step or two beyond the usual. It is largely through the spoken word that we communicate with each other, develop understanding, exchange knowledge and find mutually acceptable goals. Through effective public speaking we can encourage, teach, entertain and inspire others.

Effective speaking is simply persuasive conversation developed and adapted to fit the occasion, further a special purpose, and suit the people who listen.

Guidelines for effective speaking

- **Be familiar with the place:** Reach the venue before time, and be familiar with the position of the podium, microphone, arrangement of the stage and the seating arrangement for the audience.
- **Try to know your audience:** Greet the audience when you arrive. It will help you to establish a rapport with them.
- **Practice your speech:** Practice your speech repetitively. It will help you minimise your nervousness and will make you comfortable in front of the audience.
- **Be relaxed:** Try to remove fear by deep breathing and simple exercises, and feel relaxed.
- **Focus on the message:** Ignore anxieties and any other distractions, and focus only on the message you are trying to deliver.
- **Be confident:** Control your nervousness and transform it in to enthusiasm. Enthusiasm generates confidence.

3.2.3 Interview Skills

Interview situations are a part of our everyday life. It is a situation in which one person asks specific questions to another person for some definite purpose.

> The word 'interview' (inter-view) means 'view between'. It suggests a meeting between two or more persons to get a view of each other or to know each other.

It is a method or tool to measure the suitability of a person for some task, to collect or provide some information, to know someone's view to convince someone or even to solve some problem.

> **Example of some interview situations**
> - A father asks his son about his failure in exam.
> - Journalists ask some specific questions to a minister.
> - A police officer interrogates a criminal.
> - A doctor collects information from a patient.
> - An employer evaluates a candidate for a job.

Purpose and types of interview

❖ To select a person for some task (Job Interview)
❖ To provide/ collect some information (Information interview)
❖ To monitor the progress or to evaluate certain qualities/ achievements of someone (Evaluation interview)
❖ To gather the other person's views/ opinions (Survey)
❖ To clear differences between two person or two parties (conflict resolution interview)
❖ To remove someone from a job (Exit interview)

A job Interview is one of the tools used by an employer to evaluate the candidate. The skill of performing well in interviews plays a decisive role in determining the career of any job-aspirant.

> **Job interviews have become complex and more systematic these days due to**
> - Increasing numbers of candidates for fewer jobs
> - Growing competition in the business world
> - Changing expectations of the employers
> - Change in interview process

Moreover, the awareness that 'he/she is being evaluated' makes the candidate more self-conscious and nervous. Only adequate qualifications and work experience are not sufficient for getting selected for a job. The candidate has to convince the employer about his suitability for the job by showing his attitude, abilities and skills. Hence, proper preparation is required to become successful in interview.

Types of Job interviews

The types of job interviews are campus interview, on–site interview, face-to-face interview, panel or committee interview, behavioural interview, telephonic interview, etc.

➢ **Campus Interview**

Campus interview is very common these days. Companies contact the educational institute, express their interest of recruitment and announce eligibility criteria, date and time in advance. On the day of the interview, the recruiters provide basic information regarding their company and the selection process.

➢ **Face-to-face interview**

In a face-to-face interview, one person evaluates the other by asking questions. Most of the job interviews are face-to-face.

In such situations, the focus of the candidate should be on the person asking questions. The candidate has to maintain proper eye contact, and respond carefully to the questions asked. Here, the aim of the candidate is to establish rapport with the interviewer and show him/her that his/her attitude and qualifications will benefit the organisation.

➢ **Behavioural Interview**

This is the common type of job interview in the modern workplace. It is also known as a competency-based interview.

This type of interview is based on the notion that a candidate's past behaviour is a good indicator of future performance. Here, the interviewer asks the candidate to recall specific instances they faced with a set of cirsumstances, and how they reacted.

> **Typical behavioural interview questions**
> - Tell me about a project you worked on where the requirements changed midstream. What did you do?
> - Tell me about a time when you took the lead on a project. What did you do?
> - Describe the worst project you worked on.
> - Describe a time you had to work with someone you didn't like.
> - Tell me about a time when you had to stick by a decision you had made.

➢ Panel or committee interview

In this type of interview, the candidate is interviewed by a panel or an interview committee. This is the most common type of interview in academic and proessional sectors. In this type of interview different modes are used in conducting the interview as discussed below.

❖ Presentation mode

The candidate is asked to make a presentation before the panel on a given topic. It is often used in academic or sales – related interviews.

❖ Role Mode

Each panelist asks questions related to a specific role of the position. For example, one panelist may ask technical questions, one may ask management related questions, while one may ask customer service related questions, etc.

❖ Rapid fire mode

The candidate faces questions from the panelists in rapid succession, to test his/her ability to handle stress filled situation.

➢ Case Interview

In this type of interview, the candidate is expected to demonstrate his/her problem solving skills. The interviewer outlines a situation or provides a case study, and asks the candidate to formulate a plan that deals with the problem. The interviewers are looking for how the candidate applies his/her knowledge and skills to a real-life situation.

➢ Telephone interview

Many organisations conduct interviews over telephone to narrow down a list of candidates. Telephonic interviews may also be used as a preliminary stage of interviewing process for the candidates who live away from the job site. It is important to understand that this interview is as important as a face-to-face interview. The candidate has to focus on the conversation, listen to the questions carefully before giving the answer. While facing a telephonic interview, the candidate should keep a copy of his/her resume in hand as a reference.

Tips and techniques for interviews

Interviewing for a job can be an unpleasant experience for many people. One may feel uncomfortable on facing unexpected questions.

With the right tips and techniques and plenty of practice one can become a master of sharing his/her views with potential employers and presenting his/herself effectively. Following are some tips and techniques for facing interview with confidence.

- ❖ **Preparation**
  - ✓ Before you walk into any interview, know about the company and the position you have applied for.
  - ✓ Identify your strengths and weaknesses and prepare accordingly.
  - ✓ Go through your resume twice or thrice and collect some ideas for a few important questions that the employer is likely to ask.

> **To prepare, think about how you would answer the following questions**
> Tell me about your professional background
> Review your career, education and other strengths.
> What do you know about our organisation?
> Why are you interested in this position?
> How would you describe your personality?

- **Dress for success**
  - ✓ Take time for a pleasant appearance, have neatly trimmed hair, and clean shave.
  - ✓ Wear formal dress preferably soft coloured shirt and trouser.
  - ✓ Try to look professional.
- ❖ **Make a good first impression**
  - ✓ Make a good first impression; don't be late for the interview.
  - ✓ Greet the interviewer with a smile. If you know his/her name, be s ure you know its correct pronunciation and spelling.
  - ✓ Shake hands with a firm grip, but not too firm grip
  - ✓ Show enthusiasm and confidence in your voice and posture.
- ❖ **Pay attention to body language**
  - ✓ Watch your posture; sit up straight, don't slump.
  - ✓ Rest your hands on the table to help ensure correct posture.
  - ✓ Avoid excessive hand gestures.
  - ✓ Make a good eye contact and maintain it throughout the interview.
- ❖ **During the interview**
  - ✓ Keep a smiling face and respond the interviewing panel appropriately.
  - ✓ Listen attentively to the questions.
  - ✓ Use professional language; avoid slang.
  - ✓ Ask for clarification if you do not understand a question.
  - ✓ Give complete answers and use specific examples whenever possible.
  - ✓ Use illustrations, descriptions, and statistics to support your answer.

- ✓ Answer questions with honesty and sincerity.
- ✓ Be aware of the time allocated.
- ✓ Do not criticise former employers, faculty or associates
- ✓ Avoid talking about personal problems.

❖ **After the interview**
- ✓ Make a phone call or send a small letter of thanks to the employer for the interview opportunity.
- ✓ Keep in touch with the employer to keep your relations alive with them.

3.2.4 Listening Skill

Listening is one of the most important skills of communication. It is equally important for common people as well as for professionals like engineers, doctors, lawyers, managers, teachers and others.

Listening is the first stage of learning a language. All of us have learnt and mastered our mother-tongue by listening to it from the people with whom we live and grow. This is how a child learns the language and this is why experts say that "One can learn any languages if he/she listens to it sufficiently". This is more so in case of professionals because listening is an important component of decision-making and problem-solving. It is a proven fact that professionals spend almost half of their formal time listening to the people around them- higher management, subordinates, dealers, clients, suppliers, creditors, bankers, government agencies, non-government organisation and consumers.

We hear many sounds around us all the time but we do not pay attention to all of them carefully; while we are standing in the market we hear all sorts of sounds– sellers, blowing of vehicle-horns, barking of dogs, chats of people, chirping of birds and so on. We simply hear them. This is called 'hearing'.

Now, imagine that you are in conversation with your teacher. You will pay serious attention to every word that he/she speaks and you will also mark his/her facial expressions and gestures. In short, you will listen and understand the words as well as the intention behind the words. Thus, receiving, interpreting, understanding and responding to the important sounds is called *'listening'*.

It is a joint responsibility of both speaker and listener to contribute his/her share for effective listening. It has the following qualities:

- Healthy interpersonal relations between speaker and listener
- Appropriate medium, time and place of conversation.
- Common language known to both
- Respect for each other's feelings and needs
- Brief and to-the -point content
- Proper facial expressions gestures and postures.

Process of Listening

Listening is a process of receiving, interpreting, evaluating and responding to spoken words. It involves recognising what is said and comprehending the matter, i.e. understanding the sounds spoken by the speaker. This means that in listening, understanding of both the words and the speaker's intention are equally important. Listening is a conscious activity which requires complete involvement of the listener. Any kind of distraction may result into loss of information, misunderstanding or misinterpretation.

Listening involves activities like reception and decoding of verbal message sent by the speaker, but careful efforts must also be made to interpret them correctly. In addition, listening skill also involves the recognition of some other signals like pause, stress, tone, and rhythm pattern. The whole listening process passes through four stages

- Sensing   - The listener hears the sound with attention.
- Decoding - The listener decodes or interprets the message.
- Evaluating - The listener evaluates the message.
- Response - The listener responds to the message.

➤ Sensing

Sensing is the first step of the listening process. Sensing means physical reception of sound waves by our ears. In other words, it is a physical hearing of the message. In this stage, the listener hears the sounds and concentrates on them in order to receive the message. This stage happens naturally in every hearing situation.

➤ Decoding

It is the second step of the listening process in which the listener interprets the received signal. This means the listener changes the coded message into meaningful information. This is what we mean by understanding the spoken language. Interpretation of a verbal message may be influenced by our social, educational, psychological, economical, cultural professional and intellectual backgrounds.

➤ Evaluating

In this stage, the receiver evaluates the significance of the received message; evaluation of the message helps the receiver draw appropriate conclusions for feedback to the sender.

In order to evaluate a verbal message correctly, we separate facts from opinions, relevant information from irrelevant one, ideas from examples, and correct information from incorrect one. Along with this, we focus on clearly communicated information as well as information suggested but not communicated directly.

Further, the listener also evaluates the intention and attitude of the speaker and frames a parallel message to be sent as a feedback.

➤ Response

Response is the reaction of the listener to the message. It is the last stage of the listening process. The response largely depends on the evaluation of the message by the listener. If the message has been analysed, interpreted and evaluated correctly, the response will be appropriate. The response makes the communication complete and effective as it clarifies the message and helps the two speakers to know whether the message has been understood or not.

Types of Listening

Listening falls into several categories. These categories are created according to the objective (purpose) and function of listening. The list of the possible types of listening can be very long, but five of them are discussed below with examples. Let's have a look at them.

The Most common types of listening
- Discriminative listening
- Comprehensive listening
- Critical listening
- Appreciative listening
- Empathetic listening

> **Discriminative listening**

This is the most basic type of listening. The objective of discriminative listening is to understand clearly the sound and the visual stimuli. Here, the listener concentrates on the non-verbal elements like the speaker's tone, pitch, word stress, volume facial expression, gesture etc. in addition to the words used by the speaker.

In discriminative listening, the listener's major focus is on meaning which helps him/her decide the further step.

In the following examples the listener tries to understand speaker's intention rather than words.

Examples of discriminative listening
- A clever customer listens to the salesman explaining a product.
- Suppose a speaker is lying, the listener senses that lie.
- Parent listening to a child about an incident in school.
- Listening to an ambulance siren or horn of the vehicle.

> **Comprehensive listening**

The term 'comprehend' means to 'understand' or to 'learn'. Comprehensive listening is a very common in our everyday life. It means to listen to something in order to comprehend the meaning out of it. In comprehensive listening, the focus is to 'understand the message fully'. Through comprehensive listening, the listener gets new information or updates the existing knowledge stored in the mind.

Examples of comprehensive listening

- A student listens to his/her teacher in a classroom
- A participant listens to the expert during a seminar.
- A person listens to news on television.
- A child listens to the advice of his grandfather.
- A person listens to audio recordings at the time of an IELTS exam.
- A person listens to the host and contestants on a reality show.

> **Critical listening**

Critical listening is listening to something in order to evaluate and judge. Critical listening helps the listener frame an opinion on what is being said, and come to judgment. Judgment includes assessing strengths and weaknesses of the speaker's message. Critical listening is also called evaluative or judgmental listening.

Examples of critical listening

- A judge listens to both the lawyers in the court of law.
- Members of interview panel listen to the candidates in an interview.
- Judges listen to the participants in competitive events.

> **Appreciative listening**

In this type of listening, the listener listens for the purpose of deriving joy, pleasure or entertainment. In appreciative listening, the listener's focus is on enjoyment from what he listens to. It is self-selected listening at leisure time.

Examples of appreciative listening

- Watching comedy programmes on TV like Laughter Challenge, Tarak Mehta ka Ulta Chashma, Comedy nights with Kapil, watching movies in a theatre, listening to music, mimicry, jokes, poetry or even the speech of a great leader.

> **Empathetic listening**

Empathetic listening is also called active listening or reflective listening. It helps improve mutual understanding and trust among the people. It involves understanding the content of a message, feelings of the sender and the circumstances under which the message is given.

The listener listens to the expressed feelings and the intention of the speaker and responds to the speaker empathetically.

Empathetic Listening

Builds trust and respect, enables the disputants to share and release their emotions, reduces tensions, encourages the evolving of information

Example of empathetic listening

We listen to a distressed friend who wants to vent his/her emotions. A psychiatrist listens to the patients.

Modes of listening

Listening takes place in three different modes, which are:
1. Combative or competitive mode
2. Active or reflective mode
3. Passive or attentive mode.

> **Combative or competitive mode**

In certain situations, the listener pretends as if he/she is listening to the speaker but, actually he/she is simply waiting for the chance to talk. In competitive or combative mode of listening, the listener is waiting to insert his/her own comment in the discussion. Here, the listener seems interested in the speaker but, not in the understanding what the speaker is saying, actually he/she is only formulating what he/she wants to say next. Sometimes the listener opposes or even attacks the speaker by his/her comments.

Following instances may fall in this mode:

> Discussion on any political issue, debate on any topic, discussion on religious issues, discussion on any policies or decisions, etc.

> **Active or reflective mode**

Active or reflective listening is the single most useful and important listening mode. In active listening, a listener tries to understand, interpret and evaluate what he/she hears. The listener is genuinely interested in understanding what the other person is thinking, feeling, wanting or what the message means.

Here, the listener pays attention to the speakers; not only that, but he/she verifies his/her understanding with the speaker's intention by asking cross questions or using appropriate responses. Active mode of listening reflects back the main points and summary of what has been said. Following instances may fall in this mode.

- ❖ A Customer listens to an insurance agent explaining insurance policy.
- ❖ A participant in a workshop listens to the presentation.
- ❖ A doctor listens to his/her patient.

> **Passive or attentive mode**

Passive listening is listening without reacting to the message. This mode allows full room to the speaker without facing any kind of interruption. A passive listener seems to be attentive to the speaker but does not give any feedback to him/her. Here, the listener does not verify his/her understanding with the speaker's intention following instances may fall in this mode.

- ❖ Nowadays, students listen passively to their teachers in classrooms.
- ❖ The audience listens to the guest speaker in any inaugural or valedictory function.
- ❖ Listening to the speech of a political leader at the time of election campaign.
- ❖ While watching any movie, the viewers listen to the dialogues of the actor.

Barriers to effective listening

We know that many problems in life arise due to improper listening. This results in misinterpretation, misunderstanding, wrong actions, sour relations and so on. If we analyse the listening situations carefully, we find that certain specific reasons and habits of people are often causing such problems. The following is a brief discussion of such reasons and habits, which are also considered as barriers to effective listening.

- ❖ Environmental distractions
- ❖ Listener's ego
- ❖ Assumptions
- ❖ Close-mindedness
- ❖ Language Differences

➤ **Environmental distractions**

This means any environmental factor that distracts the attention of an individual or group from the speakers. It is the lack of ability to pay attention, perhaps due to the lack of interest in the speaker. These distractions come from both the external sources and the internal sources.

External distractions can include the disturbance in electronic gadgets like public address systems, telephone networks, music players, television, traffic noise, physical or mental distance with the speaker, etc.	**Internal distractions** can be absent-mindedness, lack of interest, lack of attention, restlessness, negative attitude etc.

➤ **Listener's ego**

Another type of listening barrier is our pride or ego. Most often, we let our pride or ego take over the conversation. We think that we are already smart enough not to have to listen to other people. We think that we are better than other people and that we have nothing more to learn from them.

➤ **Assumptions**

Assumptions is something that is accepted to be true without any proof and from which a conclusion can be drawn. Quite often, when we make assumptions, we create conclusions in our mind without even considering the thoughts and feelings of the other person. Sometimes our assumptions disturb us in listening, and thereby, we create a gap in communication and unresolved problems.

➤ **Close-mindedness**

Another listening barrier to effective conversation is close-mindedness. Close-mindedness is being stubbornly unreceptive to new ideas. Close-mindedness results in intolerance of the beliefs and opinions of others.

> When we think that we have all answers, and the things we know are always the right answers, then our mind will be close to new ideas.

> Language differences

Friends, if a listener is not familiar with the language used by the speaker, he/she finds it difficult to understand to the message. Sometimes a speaker's language itself hinders the communication. Example:

> The language spoken by a non-native speaker, e.g. A Tamilian speaks Gujarati.
> Here, interference of speaker's mother tongue prevents the listener from listening correctly.

Tips for effective listening

Listen to the speaker attentively

Sit up straight or lean forward slightly to show your attentiveness through body language.

Maintain eye contact

Maintain eye contact to the degree that you both (listener and speaker) feel comfortable.

Minimise external distractions

Turn off the TV, put down your book or magazine and concentrate on the message.

Respond appropriately to show that you understand

Murmur ('uh-huh' and 'um-hmm') and nod. Raise your eyebrows. Say words such as 'yes', 'ok', 'really'. Interesting, or ask the speaker 'what did you do then?' what did he say?' etc.

Focus only on what the speaker is saying

Stop talking to yourself. Focus your attention on the message.

3.2.5 Group Discussion

Business organisations are growing larger in size, and their activities and people working in them are also increasing in number. This is why organisations need people who can interact in small groups and offer help in solving problems. 'Teamwork' and 'group communication' have become very necessary skills today, giving rise to participative management.

Group communication is a regular event in business organisations for decision making and problem-solving. The skill of group communication is necessary for taking part in meetings, seminars, conventions and conferences. This is why employers check group communication skills while offering jobs.

Group discussion (GD) is a form of oral group communication. It is a way of developing, sharing and discussing ideas among the individuals of a group on a specific topic. As discussed earlier, group discussions are used in two situations.

1. In companies, for problem-solving and decision-making
2. During interview to check group communication skills of job seekers.

In the second situation, it is sometimes a primary stage of the selection process of an employee in an organisation. Thus GD is a widely used tool in recruitment and admission when the number of candidates is large.

Let's see how group discussion is used as a tool during the selection process.

In a group discussion for selection or admission, the group of candidates is given a topic or a situation, given a few minutes to think about that topic, and asked to discuss it among themselves for 15-20 minutes

Group discussion assesses
- Communication skills
- Ability to initiate the discussion
- Knowledge and ideas regarding the given subject
- Ability to work in a team
- Capability to co-ordinate and lead
- Reasoning ability, creativity, flexibility

Topics of GD

Group discussion can be divided into two broad categories.
- Topic based GD
- Case based GD

Topic based group discussion can be carried out with three different kinds of topics, which are.
- Factual topics
- Controversial Topics
- Abstract Topics

➢ **Factual topics**

Factual topics are about any practical matter, about which a candidate is expected to be aware of. These can be topics based on current issue like politics, sports and other national or international events. A factual topic for discussion gives a candidate a chance to prove that he is aware of the facts of current national and / or international events. Following examples may fall into this category.
- Education policy in India
- Status of the aged people in the nation
- Tourism in India

➢ **Controversial topics**

Controversial topics are argumentative in nature having many controversies and pros and cons. They are meant to generate controversy. These topics test especially the maturity level (personal and emotional sensitivity) of the candidate. Following examples may fall into this category.

- The India – US nuclear deal – is it beneficial or not?
- Girls do well in the academics; there should not be any reservations for them.

➤ Abstract topics

Abstract topics are about intangible things which are difficult to describe exactly. Often these topics are not given for discussion, but their possibility cannot be overlooked. These topics test candidate's imagination and creativity following examples may fall in this category.

- Honesty is the best policy
- Are animals better than human beings?
- Bright red colour excites our emotions

➤ Case-study based topics

Here, a case study is used for the discussion instead of a topic. The case study tries to create a real-life situation. Candidates will be provided information about the situation and will be asked as a group to resolve the situation. In a case-study, there are no correct answers or perfect solutions. The objective of the case-study is to get the candidates to think about the situation from various angles.

Features and assessment of selection process group discussion

- ❖ The discussion group is generally small (8 to 10 candidates) and the time is fixed (25 or 30 minutes).
- ❖ GD is used as a medium to understand the participant's strength and weaknesses; it reveals the participants' true personality and leadership quality.
- ❖ There is no leader in the group, and the candidates sit in circle, block or 'U' shape.
- ❖ The rules and evaluation process are explained to the candidates.
- ❖ Once the case or topic is presented, candidates are given some time for thinking.
- ❖ Signal is given for starting and ending the discussion.
- ❖ The common topics for group discussion are politics, sports, science, trade and commerce, industry and technology.
- ❖ The candidates are evaluated on the basis of behaviour in group, ability of oral and non verbal communication, leadership qualities, knowledge of the topic, logical thinking, power of argument, skill of convincing others, skill of patient listening, creative thinking.

How to participate effectively in GD? (Do and Don'ts)

- ❖ **While taking part in GD**
    - Listen to others carefully and wait for your turn patiently.
    - Talk with confidence and self-assurance.
    - Do not become aggressive but put forward your points logically
    - Do not say anything in contrast to what you have already said
    - Present genuine points and support them by substantial reasoning
    - Put across your points with logic and with relevant examples.
    - Do not hurt anyone's self-respect with your statements.

- Use the right words in your arguments (words make friends but right word at the right time make the best friend)
- Do not engage yourself in sub-group conversations.
- Do not interrupt any other person while he/she is speaking
- Be empathetic towards the other participants of GD.
- Do not make fun of any participant even if his/her argument is invalid or incorrect.
- Do not use or repeat irrelevant material.
- Talk to the participants and not to the examiners.
- Do not be shy, nervous, or isolated from the GD.

3.2.6 Oral Presentation

In a student's life and in business or working life, one has to face situations in which one is required to make oral presentations on different topics before groups of people. Students have to prepare oral presentations before their teachers and evaluators, research scholars present the outcome of their research before a panel of judges, business executives make oral presentations on a new idea, or product before customer, the top management, government agencies, etc. Thus, the skill of making successful oral presentations is essential for everyone whether student or professional. Making a memorable and successful oral presentation requires careful planning, systematic arrangement of ideas, good computer skills, sound command of language, and effective skills of interpersonal communication.

Oral presentation is an organised way to put across our ideas, opinions, beliefs, etc. before a group of people. It is an important skill which can be developed by regular practice. It is a systematic form of communication and therefore it has a logical beginning, middle, and end.

Components of an Oral presentation

Have you ever seen an oral presentation without an audience or an oral presentation without a presenter? Surely your answer would be NO! Similarly it is not possible to make an oral presentation without an idea or topic. There are three basic components of an oral presentation, which are:

- Audience
- Presenter
- Idea to be presented.

In the absence of any one of them, an oral presentation is not possible.

Planning for effective oral presentation

Oral presentation should be prepared with careful planning to make it more effective. A presenter should think about the following matters before he/she starts preparing his/her oral presentation.

> - The purpose of oral presentation is to inform, to persuade, to influence, to raise awareness, to educate, or to entertain.
> - The audience in terms of personality, age, education, prior knowledge about the topic, etc.
> - Outline of content for the oral presentation.
> - The place and facilities available for oral presentation.
> - Possible time allotted for the oral presentation.
> - Possible strategies for the delivery of oral presentation.

➢ **The Purpose of oral presentation**

Before preparing the oral presentation, it is essential for the presenter to be aware about the purpose of it. To think about the purpose of the oral presentation, the presenter should ask himself/ herself the basic questions: **"Why am I making this oral presentation?'** The answer to this question provides the purpose of the oral presentation, which guides him/her in its preparation. Look at the following possible purposes of oral presentation.

> **To inform:** To tell the audience about particular facts
> **To influence:** To change how issue is perceived or understood by the audience.
> **To educate:** To teach someone, especially using the formal system of Interaction.
> **You can also think about some more possible purposes!!!**

➢ **Know Your audience**

Knowledge about the audience of the oral presentation helps presenter in selecting content and effective strategy of the oral presentation. The audience of the oral presentation will have their own experience, views, interests and level of knowledge. Therefore, the presenter should think about these factors and prepare the oral presentation accordingly. Here, the presenter should ask him/herself: **'Who are the people making up the audience of my oral presentation?'** The answer helps the presenter know the audience before preparing the oral presentation.

➢ **Select your content**

After knowing the purpose and the audience of the oral presentation, the presenter selects the content for his/her oral presentation. Here, he/she should ask himself/herself the question: **'What am I going to say to my audience?'** the answer will help the presenter select the content for his/her oral presentation, on the basis of the purpose and the audience's needs and expectations.

➢ **Place and time**

While planning for oral presentation, the presenter thinks about the place and time of his/her oral presentation. Answers to questions like: **'Where will I be making my oral presentation?'** and **'How much time have I been allotted?'** give the presenter hints for the selection of content and devices to be used in the oral presentation. The preparation of the oral presentation depends on the knowledge of place and context of the oral presentation.

Mode of presentation

Finally, the presenter thinks about the delivery of presentation. Answer to the question: **'How shall I put my ideas to the audience?'** helps him/her define a strategy for the delivery of his/her oral presentation. The presenter should think about how to hold, retain or achieve maximum attention of the audience during the oral presentation.

It has been proven that three factors play a major role in holding the attention of the audience in the oral presentation. These factors are **words**, **style** and **body language**.

Here, **words** means the verbal content selected. ***Style*** means the way the speaker uses the words which include Para-linguistic features such as pause, stress, tone, rhythm etc. ***Body Language*** means non-verbal communication like facial expressions, gestures and postures.

Steps for preparing oral presentation

There are some basic steps which need to be followed at the time of preparing an oral presentation.

❖ Research for the content

To prepare an effective oral presentation, the first thing the presenter needs to do is research for the content of his/her presentation. He/she may have some prior information about the topic, but it is also essential to have some critical facts and additional relevant information, which he/she may get from a variety of sources like friends and colleagues, textbooks, library and the internet. This is called the **Information gathering stage** of the preparation.

❖ Selection of content

The next step of preparing an oral presentation is to select the content of the presentation according to the defined objective and audience analysis. From the collected material during the information gathering stage, the presenter selects only what is relevant to the subject of his/her presentation, meets the needs and expectations of the audience, and can be presented within the allotted time. After careful selection of the content for the presentation, the presenter organiser his/her points in a proper order which can fulfill the objective of presentation.

❖ Decide the strategy

A strategy of the presentation needs to be decided by the presenter for the smooth course of presentation which helps him/her hold the attention of the audience on the topic.

❖ Writing a script

The ideas collected should be organised and written in a proper and logical order, so that they can be presented in an effective manner. The points in the script can be written on cue cards which the presenter can carry with him. This is a much better strategy than taking entire sheets of written text.

Detailed Preparation

❖ Visuals

In oral presentation, visual aids such as slides, models, objects etc. are used to elaborate the point or ideas. It is advised to prepare necessary visual aids much in advance of the presentation.

- ❖ **Handouts**

    Handout is a piece of paper which contains the main points to be discussed in the presentation. Handouts are distributed among the audience before the presentation so that the audience can attend the presentation with prior information about the points to be discussed. Prepare your handout carefully as the participant of your presentation will take it home with them after the presentation.

- ❖ **Feedback forms**

    Feedback forms allow the participants to make their comments about the oral presentation. Feedback by the audience helps the presenter know about his/her performance on the presentation. The presenter should prepare his/her feedback forms in advance and distribute them to the participants at the end of the presentation. The following points can be included in a feedback form.

    ✓ The opinion of the audiences about the speaker.
    ✓ Suggestions for improvement in the presentation.
    ✓ Prior expectations of the audiences from the presentation and satisfaction from the content of the session.
    ✓ Evaluation of the speaker on various points such as: delivery of content, use of visuals, behaviour, overall performance of the presenter, etc.
    ✓ Overall usefulness of the presentation.
    ✓ Any other comments.

- ❖ **Practice**

    We all know that practice makes the skill permanent. The most important factor to make the oral presentation a grand success is **Practice.... Practice.... And practice!!!**

    Making a good presentation is not an easy task. Prior practice will help the presenter when he/she is on the stage. The Presenter should practice with his/her voice and visuals. During practice, a presenter should also concentrate on the time factor. Repetitive practice of the presentation boosts up the confidence of the presenter. The presenter should pretend that he/she is in front of an audience. The presenter should make sure that he/she is addressing the entire room, not just the first few rows or a specific side of the room. The presenter should try to make his/her movements meaningful; doesn't just move for the sake of moving.

    > In the initial phases, practice is important to remove the element of fear. In the latter stages it helps in brushing up the content and style of presentation and reveals your self – confidence.

Boredom factors in presentation

During oral presentation, certain factors crop up and these factors cause negative effect on the process of presentation. They distract attention of the audience from the presentation and decrease its effectiveness. The factors playing the role of obstacles in the presentation are known as *boredom factors*. Following is the list of boredom factors of oral presentation.

- ❖ Lack of enthusiasm.
- ❖ Lack of preparation.
- ❖ Flat or monotone voice.
- ❖ Static presentation of facts and figures without real-life examples.
- ❖ Overuse of words such as: like, um, uh, ok, you know.
- ❖ Absence of humour in the speech.
- ❖ Lack of appropriate facial expressions.
- ❖ Unorganised content.
- ❖ Large audience in small room.
- ❖ Inappropriate use of language.
- ❖ Improper planning.
- ❖ Overuse of time.
- ❖ Inappropriate and unorganised visual content.

Points to Remember

- Soft skills are personal attributes that enhance an individual's interactions, job performance and career prospects. Soft skill of an individual plays an important role in the success of an organisation. Specifically organisations who interact personally with the customers, need to train their employees to employ their soft skills.
- Soft skills are the kind of skills needed to perform jobs where job requirements are defined in terms of expected outcomes
- **Importance of Soft skills**
    1. Improves communication skills
    2. Develops overall personality
    3. Team Building
    4. Problem solving ability
    5. Customer service skills
    6. Entrepreneurship skills
    7. Leadership skills
    - **Grooming** is the process of making yourself looks neat, attractive and presentable. In simple words grooming means the things which you do to make yourself and your appearance appear tidy and pleasant.
    - **Business etiquette** is a set of rules that govern the way people interact with one another in business, with customers, suppliers, with inside or outside bodies. It is all about conveying the right image and behaving in an appropriate way. Etiquette refers to behaving in a socially responsible way.
    - Etiquette refers to guidelines which control the way a responsible individual should behave in the society.

- **Types of Etiquette**
  1. Social Etiquette
  2. Corporate Etiquette
  3. Meeting Etiquette
  4. Telephone Etiquette
  5. Business Etiquette
  - **Effective Speaking:** Effective speaking is simply persuasive conversation developed and adapted to fit the occasion, further a special purpose, and suit the people who listen.
3. **Interview Skills:** The word 'interview' (inter-view) means 'view between'. It suggests a meeting between two or more persons to get a view of each other or to know each other. It is a method or tool to measure the suitability of a person for some task, to collect or provide some information, to know someone's view to convince someone or even to solve some problem.
- **The purpose of interview are**
  - To select a person for some task (Job Interview)
  - To provide/ collect some information (Information interview)
  - To monitor progress or to evaluate certain qualities/ achievements of someone (Evaluation interview)
  - To gather the other person's views/ opinions (Survey)
  - To clear differences between two person or two parties (conflict resolution interview)
  - To remove someone from a job (Exit interview)
- Types of job interviews are campus interview, on-site interview, face-to-face interview, panel or committee interview, behavioural interview, telephonic interview etc
  - **Listening** is one of the most important skills of communication. It is equally important for both common people as well as professionals like engineers, doctors, lawyers, managers, teachers and others. Listening is the first stage of learning a language.
  - Listening is a process of receiving, interpreting, evaluating and responding to spoken words.
  - The whole listening process passes through four stages
  - Sensing   -   The listener hears the sound with attention.
  - Decoding   -   The listener decodes or interprets the message.
  - Evaluating -   The listener evaluates the message.
  - Response   -   The listener responds to the message.

- **The most common types of listening are**
  - Discriminative listening
  - Comprehensive listening
  - Critical listening
  - Appreciative listening
  - Empathetic listening
- Listening takes place in three different modes, which are:
  1. Combative or competitive mode
  2. Active or – reflective mode
  3. Passive or attentive mode.
- **Barriers to effective listening**
  - Environmental distractions
  - Listener's ego
  - Assumptions
  - Close-mindedness
  - Language Differences
- **Group Discussion** is a form of oral group communication. It is a way of developing, sharing and discussing ideas among the individuals of a group on a specific topic.
- **Group discussion assesses the candidates'**
  - Communication skills
  - Ability to initiate the discussion.
  - Knowledge and ideas regarding the given subject.
  - Ability to work in a team
  - Capability to co-ordinate and lead
  - Reasoning ability, creativity, flexibility
- Oral Presentation is an organised way to put across our ideas, opinions, beliefs, etc. before a group of people. It is an important skill which can be developed by regular practice. It is a systematic form of communication and therefore it has a logical beginning, middle, and end.
- There are three basic required components of an oral presentation, which are:
  - Audience
  - Presenter
  - Ideas to be presented
- **Steps for preparing oral presentation**
  - Research for the content
  - Selection of content

- Decide the strategy
  - Writing a script
  - Detailed Preparation
  - Visuals
  - Handouts
  - Practice
- The factors playing the role of obstacles in the process of presentation are known as boredom factor. These factors are
  - Lack of enthusiasm
  - Lack of preparation
  - Flat or monotone voice
  - Static presentation of facts and figures without real-life examples.
  - Overuse of words such as : like, um, uh, ok, you know
  - Absence of humor in the speech.
  - Lack of appropriate facial expressions.
  - Unorganised content.
  - Large audience in small room.
  - Inappropriate use of language
  - Improper planning
  - Overuse of time
  - Inappropriate and unorganised visual content

FREQUENTLY ASKED QUESTIONS FROM UNIVERSITY OF PUNE EXAMINATIONS

1. State the barriers in listening. **[April 2006]**
2. State the types of listeners **[April 2007, 2009]**
3. Explain the techniques of effective speech **[Oct. 2007]**
4. What do you mean by listening? Explain in detail the principles of listening. **[Oct. 2007]**
5. Define the term listening. Describe the detail types of listeners. **[April 2010]**
6. Define the term 'Soft skill'. Explain the elements of Soft-skill. **[Oct. 2011]**
7. What is listening? Explain the principles of barriers of good listening. **[April 2012, 2013]**
8. Explain in detail the techniques of an interview. **[April 2013]**

Chapter ... **4**

BUSINESS LETTERS

Contents ...
- 4.1 Introduction
- 4.2 Importance of Business Letters
- 4.3 Qualities or Essentials of Good Business Letters
- 4.4 Physical Appearance
- 4.5 Layout / Style of Business Letters
- • Points to Remember
- • Frequently Asked Questions from University of Pune Examination

Learning Objectives ...
- To understand and study the importance of business letters
- To learn the qualities and essentials of a good business letter
- To learn the physical appearance and layout of business letters and finally to see some specimen letters

4.1 Introduction

Business letters are the life-breath of business. Despite the availability of telephone, fax, etc., which are very fast, conventional mail is still very popular. People like the feel of a good old "letter" in hand. It also increases the reach of a business house.

A letter is written to reach where you cannot reach yourself, and say what you cannot say yourself personally. Thus a letter plays the role of your representative or ambassador. All the qualities of a good ambassador – the polish and the courtesy, the knowledge and the convincing power – have to be there in a good business letter.

The competition in today's business world is described as "unreal" – too hard to believe. Those who have survived the competition and made it to the top are the ones who mastered, among other things, the art of writing good letters. Moreover, it is found that nearly 70% of the world's international business correspondence is in English. It follows some conventions which have to be learnt. These may of course change from time to time and from country to country. We have to up-date ourselves in this matter.

4.2 Importance of Business Letters

Here is an analysis of the reasons why a business letter is valuable.

(i) **Drafting at convenience:** A letter can be composed at leisure and at any period of time, revised and edited before the presentation. In this respect it differs from an oral presentation. It can be read by the recipient at his leisure, and can make his own markings on the message received. Successful businessmen are good communicators with a mastery of writing business letters.

(ii) **Reaches far and wide:** Within town and out of it, within the country or abroad, a letter reaches the target with much convenience. Through letters, a businessman can reach thousands of persons located at thousands of places.

(iii) **A record for the purpose of law:** A written record is useful in law and for clarifying matters in the event of a dispute. Oral deals can be "airy" whereas a written record is solid evidence. That is why oral or telephonic discussions are confirmed through letters.

(iv) **A record for reference:** A letter can be kept by the recipient for reference at a later date and for drafting a reply. Instead of relying on memory alone, one can see the matter in black and white. A letter can be read in conjunction with other documents or with a chain of the previous letters.

(v) **Solidifies a business brand:** A decent letter helps to establish a business relationship which can be developed further with future deals. An oral conversation is heard only once, whereas a letter may be read many times, over days and months. Ongoing letters to customers, dealers etc. keep the relationship warm.

(vi) **Helps to expand Business:** Apart from the convenience of reaching remote places, letters enable the writer to explore new prospects in new territories. Sales letters can go in large numbers and do wonders for the sellers.

(vii) **Saves money in communication:** Personal conferences and meetings are expensive to arrange. If the same job can be done through a letter, it is better to do so. Letters are cost – effective in one more way. They save the hassles that may arise in a faulty oral presentation. Phrases frequently required can be saved and used again and again.

(viii) **Convenient for giving unpleasant news:** Sometimes unpleasant news can be given with diplomacy in a letter, e.g. a sweet NO. On some occasions, the receiver's oral reaction may be an outburst. A letter can explain the full situation of the "no" which helps to cool tempers. A letter also gives the recipient the time to think before reacting, which is a major courtesy.

In short, a letter is a neutral third party, a messenger for you, offering its own advantages over other means of communication.

4.3 Essentials of a Good Business Letter

Here we discuss the principles of letter writing, which have to be mastered in the spirit. A thorough study of these can make you sought – after letter writer and a successful entrepreneur.

There are eight C's of good business letter writing: correctness, completeness, clarity, conciseness, courtesy, consideration, concreteness, and convincing power.

(i) Correctness: The letter should contain correct information. The facts and figures need to be ascertained from the source before committing them to paper. The spellings need to be correct, the manners correct (viz. respect shown according to the position of the recipient). The grammar and punctuation need to be according to the standard usage. In real-life business situations, many letters get wisely rejected on account of the errors they contain, because to send a wrongly worded or addressed letter is to invite embarrassment and trouble.

(ii) Completeness: Enough time and attention needs to be given to make the contents in order to fulfil the intent of the letter. The terms and conditions of sale, for example, need to be fully stated. Cool editing and comprehensive thinking is required for this purpose. All enclosures of the letter should be duly attached. The dispatcher also has a role to play in this. The letter should be numbered, dated and signed.

(iii) Clarity: The letter should be worded in a clear language and be free from all ambiguity (double meaning). For example, in America the date 2/6/2006 means 6th February. Hence a letter going to U.S.A should spell the name of the month. We can write "6th February 2006". Long paragraphs and uncommon words, dead phrases and foreign language words reduce the clarity of a letter. It is best to read a lot of good letters from text – books or actual correspondence to see how the meaning is made clear.

(iv) Conciseness: Conciseness or brevity is brought into letter writing at two levels: matter and language. All extraneous information needs to be removed from the letter. Sometimes a single line of acknowledgement or thanks is enough to make an entire letter. As for language, here are some examples of how longer expressions are made concise:

Long	Short
They do not have money.	They have no money.
It is a company which is very wealthy.	It is a wealthy company.
There are a great many people who have tried this instrument.	Many people have tried this instrument

(v) Courtesy: To be courteous is to be friendly in attitude and in the use of words. Apart from basic courtesies like saying "Dear Sir" and "Yours Sincerely" there are deeper courtesies that endear a letter to its receiver. Courtesy gives rise to courtesy.

Plain	More courteous
We have received your letter...	Thank you for your letter...
Your letter is blatantly wrong...	To set the record correct, we may submit that.

(vi) Consideration: With a little recasting, a letter can sometimes be more favourable to the reader. This consideration is called "You attitude," better understood through examples (see box).

We attitude	You attitude
We are happy to inform	You will be happy to know...
We shall send a free copy if we receive...	Your free copy will be sent to you if your reply...
We will renew your subscription and send our gift...	You can renew your subscription and receive your gift...

While `you` attitude is recommended in general, it is particularly relevant in sales letters. It earns the reader's confidence and goodwill. You attitude does not mean just blind repetition of the word *you* and *your*, but a judicious tilting of the content in their reader's favour. The letter should eventually show how the writer is genuinely interested in the reader's welfare.

We attitude: We are proud to announce the launch of our new model.

A "You attitude" letter generates a more positive response. However, the use of "You attitude" does not simply mean a more frequent use of the word "you." A sentence which uses "we" and "our" also sounds nice to the reader:" We would like you to have, with our compliments, a booklet..." Thus, balancing the words "we" and "you" is a finer game.

You attitude: You will be delighted to know about our latest user-friendly new model that will serve your needs

(i) Concreteness: A business letter has to avoid approximate statements when exact ones can be given or are expected. A complaint letter can replace the phrase "loss on a large scale" by the phrase "loss of a 1000 man-hours." This can be backed up by other facts and figures. "We process loan applications speedily" can be changed to "We decide on loan applications upto ₹ 5 lakhs within 15 days."

(ii) Convincing power: Every letter sells an idea and is, to that extent, a kind of sales letter. To get appropriate action is the aim of the letter, for which all the skills of a good sales letter are to be applied. One has to state the benefit to the receiver and the reason why, and do so in an appealing language. Consider this simple request: "Please send me a brochure of your Europe tour packages as my family and friends are interested. After Nepal and Mauritius, Europe seems a logical destination." The Brochure may be expensive, but when the buying power of the letter writer and a large business prospect is offered, a Brochure is likely to materialise. In a sales letter, the endorsement of a great personality, the testimony of satisfied users, or the technical specifications of a new product are the tools used for convincing.

4.4 Physical Appearance of a Business Letter
How to give neat looks to a business letter

In public speaking, there is a saying: dress before address. Similarly, in letter writing the neatness is seen before the matter. A sloppily presented letter has to work, maybe, twice as hard to achieve its business goal.

1. **Stationery and paper:** The envelope and the paper on which the letter is typed should be worth the name of the firm, even a little better if possible. Standard paper size is A4, but a firm may get its letterhead printed on a smaller size paper also. The print layout should be artistically designed. The letter should have as few folds as possible. If a window envelope is used, the address should be clearly visible from the window (and not get covered as the address inside the window envelope should be seen).
2. **Typing:** The letter should be typed (or computer printed) with a uniform impression. Margins should be kept on all four sides, 1" to the left and right, and 1.5"at the top and bottom.
3. **Layout of parts:** All parts of the letter should be located in their allotted positions – the date, the reference no., the receiver's address, etc.
4. **Presentation:** Typing must be neat, without cancellations or corrections. The letter should be placed carefully in the centre of the page leaving equal distances.
5. **Paragraphing:** Paragraphing is necessary or essential for breaking up a composition into readable, logical and progressive units. Usually a letter has three or four paragraphs: a short opening paragraph which may have only one or two sentences, one or two longer middle paragraphs which carry the main message of the letter and a short closing paragraph, which may be only of one sentence.
6. **Packaging:** The folding of the letter must be neat and clean. The size of the folded letter must be such as to fit in envelope leaving enough space for cutting the envelope open.
7. **Address:** Address on the envelope is to be typed half way down and one third in from the left, in order to ensure that the post office stamping does not affect it. Its appearance is as important as that of the letter as it is seen before letter.

4.5 Layout / Style of Business Letters

A business letter is supposed to have a layout that impresses. Its physical appearance, that includes the quality of the paper, the arrangement of the typed/printed matter, the way it is folded and kept in the envelope, the envelope itself with the addressee's name anc address, stamping-everything communicates and passes through the receiver's mental filter.

Many companies choose their own layout. But the differences in layout are not as many as their similarities. Differences occur due to the typing/printing convention, indentinc, spacing, etc. In other words the arrangement of the different parts of a letter is known as its form or layout.

Various forms have been evolved, but the two major ones are-
- the indented form of layout.
- the block form of Layout.

There are however, at least two to three variations of these major forms.

1. Full or Complete Block Form
2. Indented Form
3. Semi-Block Form4.
4. Modified Block Form
5. Hanging Indented Form

1. Full or Complete Block Form

In this form, all the parts of the letter begin from the margin. The different parts of the letter, or even the various paragraphs, are differentiated by leaving space between each part.

Here the typist does not have to adjust to different margins for different parts of the letter. So this is the easiest form for the typist. But this form is criticised because, since all the forms begin from the left, the margin appears to be crowded and unbalanced.

Format of Full Block Form (American Style)

```
                        Company Name
                     Add, Ph, Fax Number
                    (Company Letter Head)


Ref number
Date
Inside address
Attention line
Salutation
Subject     ————————

                            Body of Letter




Subscription
Signature
Signatory's typed name
Signatory's position in the company
Company Name
Encl:
PS
Ref. Initials
```

Example of Full Block Form

NASIK ENGINEERING WORKS
6/99, Sanjibhai Marg,
Nasik

14th February, 2014,

The Financial Manager,
National Development Corporation,
36, Sardar Patel Road,
Pune – 411030.

Dear Sir,

Thank you for your Letter No. CR-143/30007 of 5 February, 2014. Your Cheque No. R1437 of 4 February, 2014 is for ₹ 1, 999.00 whereas our Bill No. MHW 10077 to 20 March 2014 was for ₹ 1,979.00. It appears to be a copying mistake; the writer of the cheque has reversed the last two digits.

I am sorry to bother you for a small amount but you will appreciate that we have to account for the goods supplied. I, therefore, hope you will not mind sending another cheque for the correct amount. I am returning your cheque No. R1437.

Yours faithfully

B.C Jaitely
(Materials Manager)

Encl: 1

Indented Form

This is the traditional form. The lines of the address and the body of the letter are indented 5 spaces from the previous lines. Every line of address has a comma at the end and the last line ends with a full stop.

This form is most suited when the letter is written in hand, as it gives a balanced appearance, but because of the indent, it wastes the time of the typist.

Format of Indented Form (British Style)

Company Letter Head
Name and Address already printed
Telegram, Cable, Telex, Telephone, Fax

Date:_____

Reference No.
Name and address of person
to whom the letter is going

*For the attention of.....
Salutation

Subject heading – not obligatory, but often used

Body of Letter

Subscription
Signature
Signatory's typed name
Signatory's position in the company
Company Name
*Encl:
*PS

(*Included only if necessary-but when used position in letter as shown above).

Example of Indented Form

Korimath Trading Company Limited
11, A, Vrundavan Road, New Delhi – 110001.

19 February, 2014

The CSV Commercial Bank Limited,
7739, Bhagat Singh Chowk,
Pune – 411030

Dear Sir,

Please refer to your Letter No. C-CS/43 of 3 February, 2014.

We are grateful that you have agreed to advance a sum of ₹ 30,000 (Rupees Thirty Thousand Only). The terms and conditions you mention are acceptable to us. We shall send you our Accounts Officer to sign the agreement at 10 a.m. on Monday, 25 February, 2014 as you have suggested.

Yours faithfully

(Signatory's Name)

Semi Block Form

This form is a compromise between the block form and the indented form. In the semi – block form, the address is written in block form with open punctuation. But in the body of the letter, the first line of every paragraph is indented 5 spaces; also the complimentary close and the signature come at the right hand corner below the body of the letter. In this form, all the parts are more or less in the block form, and so the work of the typist is made easy; but it does not save time as the main part – the body of the letter is indented.

Format of Semi Block Form

Company Letter Head
Name and Address already printed
Telegram, Cable, Telex, Telephone, Fax

Date :

Inside address :
Salutation
Ref. Our Order No.   Your Despatch No.

_____
_____
_____   } The
_____   Message
_____
_____

      Yours sincerely   Closing
      _____   Signature
      Signature   Name and
      Name   Title
      Designation

SP: CK

Example of Semi Block Form

Johnson & Johnson and Company
Yogi Hills, Pune - 411030
12 January, 2014

The Personnel Manager
Dairy Land,
Delkar Road, New Delhi – 110003.

Dear Sir,

Please refer to your letter No. P-143/7 of 7 January, 2014.

Shri. Gajul Bhasra was in our employment as an Assistant Accountant from 15 December, 2009 to 31 December, 2013. He resigned the post as the climate of this town did not suit him.

He was sincere, hardworking and efficient and we found him loyal in all circumstances. In fact, we were considering promoting him when he left. We, therefore, think him suitable for the post of an Accountant for which you are considering him.

Yours faithfully,
Rahul Sharma
(Managing Director)
Johnson & Johnson and Company

Modified Block Form

It is a widely used form as it is somewhat like the full block form. The Sender's address and date are given in the block form in the right hand corner, as also the complimentary close and the signature. All the other parts begin from the left- hand margin and are fully in the block form. This has the same advantage as the block form – that of saving the typist's time; but unlike the full block form, it looks balanced, as a few parts begin on the right.

Format of Modified Block Form

Name and Address of the Company

Ref. No		Date
Inside Name and Address		
		Complimentary Close
Salutation	Subject	Signature
		Designation

Example of Modified Block Form

BHARAT ALUMINIUM CORPORATION

303, Jahangir Road, Surat -380003

10 January, 2014

Your Reference: Letter No. 43-PC of 4 September

Our Reference: POC-30 U

The General Manager

Ambuja Cements Company Limited

Navarangpura

Kanpur – 201001.

Dear Sir,

    I regret to inform you that out of 600 bags of cement you supplied, 50 have arrived in damaged condition. They cannot be used at all in construction work. It appears the damage was caused due to inadequate protection against rains. Our storekeeper pointed this out to the truck driver immediately after unloading and he has given a signed note, accepting this position. I am enclosing this note for your information.

    I shall be grateful if you kindly make necessary adjustments in the bill. If, however, you are making supplies to someone else in this city in the near future, you may send us the replacement.

Yours faithfully,

Dilip Lahamge

(Purchase Officer)

Points to Remember

- **Importance of Business Letters**
    1. Drafting at convenience
    2. Reaches far and wide
    3. A record for the purpose of law
    4. A record for reference
    5. Solidifies a business brand
    6. Helps to expand business
    7. Save money in communication
    8. Convenient for giving unpleasant news
- There are eight C's of good business letter writing-
    - correctness,
    - completeness,
    - clarity,
    - conciseness,
    - courtesy,
    - consideration,
    - concreteness,
    - Convincing power.
- **Physical Appearance of a Business Letter**
    1. Stationery
    2. Typing
    3. Layout of parts
    4. Presentation
    5. Paragraphing
    6. Packaging
    7. Address
- The arrangement of the different parts of a letter is known as its **form** or **layout**.
- The two major forms are:
    - the indented form of layout
    - the block form of Layout.
- There are however, at least two to three variations of these major forms-
    1. Full or Complete Block Form
    2. Indented Form
    3. Semi-Block Form
    4. Modified Block Form
    5. Hanging Indented Form

FREQUENTLY ASKED QUESTIONS FROM UNIVERSITY OF PUNE EXAMINATIONS

1. Explain the functions of Business Letters. **[April 2006]**
2. Explain in detail the essential qualities of a Good Business Letter. **[April 2007]**
3. State the importance of Business Letter. **[Oct. 2007]**
4. Explain in detail the layout of Business Letter. **[Oct. 2007]**
5. Explain in detail qualities of good business letter. **[Oct. 2010]**
6. Define the term "Business Letter". Explain in detail essential qualities of a good business letter. **[April 2011]**
7. Explain the structure of Business Letter. **[April 2013]**

✱✱✱

Term - II

Chapter ... **5**

TYPES AND DRAFTING OF BUSINESS LETTERS

Contents ...

- 5.1 Enquiry and Replies
    - 5.1.1 Enquiries
    - 5.1.2 Types of Letters of Enquiry
    - 5.1.3 Drafting of Enquiry Letter
    - 5.1.4 Replies
    - 5.1.5 Sample Letters
- 5.2 Orders and Replies
    - 5.2.1 Orders
    - 5.2.2 Drafting an Order
    - 5.2.3 Examples
    - 5.2.4 Fulfilling Orders
- 5.3 Credit and Status Enquiries
    - 5.3.1 Meaning
    - 5.3.2 Sources of Status Enquiry
    - 5.3.3 Drafting Letters for Trade and Bank References
    - 5.3.4 Specimen Letters
    - 5.3.5 Replies to Status Enquiries
    - 5.3.6 Informing the Customer
    - 5.3.7 Granting Credit
    - 5.3.8 Refusing Credit
- 5.4 Sales Letters
    - 5.4.1 Introduction
    - 5.4.2 Characteristics of Sales Letters
    - 5.4.3 Advantages of Sales Letters
    - 5.4.4 Structure of Sales Letters - The Salutation
    - 5.4.5 Examples
    - 5.4.6 Conclusion

5.5 Complaint and their Adjustments
- 5.5.1 Introduction
- 5.5.2 Objectives of Compliant Letters
- 5.5.3 Circumstances on which Compliant Letters are to be sent
- 5.5.4 The Adjustment Letters
- 5.5.5 Tips for Writing an Effective Complaint Letter
- 5.5.6 Examples

5.6 Collection Letters
- 5.6.1 Meaning
- 5.6.2 Collection Series
- 5.6.3 Examples

5.7 Circular Letters
- 5.7.1 Meaning
- 5.7.2 Objectives
- 5.7.3 Occasions for Writing Circular Letters
- 5.7.4 Drafting Circular Letters
- 5.7.5 Examples of Circular Letters

- Points to Remember
- Frequently Asked Questions from University of Pune Examination

Learning Objectives ...

- To understand about enquiries and replies. Types of letters of enquiry and how to draft an enquiry letter.
- To learn about orders and replies - ways of drafting them and how to fulfill the orders
- To study about credit and status enquiries - where we will cover the means, sources, drafting the letters, replies and ways of granting credit or refusing credit.
- To study what are sales letters including characteristics, advantages, structure and with examples.
- To understand the complaint and adjustment letters
- To learn more about collection and circular letters

5.1 Enquiries and Replies

The most common letters in business are buyer's enquiries about goods and services, and sellers' replies giving information and quotations. Today, a good deal of information about goods and prices is conveyed by telephone or e-mail or fax; but in many parts of the country many do not have these facilities and prefer to use letters so that they have a document and a record for reference.

In these letters, the direct approach is used to save time. The letters are short, where formalities are not required, and you can get straight to the business.

5.1.1 Enquiries

Enquiries generally figure in the first category of letters sent by an organisation or an individual. They are, first and foremost, information seeking letters. The writer may however, also give valuable information about himself or the organisation, his or the organisation's requirements, expectations, etc. and hence this is how a letter of enquiry triggers off a two-way communication or information exchange process.

When, for example, a buyer seeks information about the price, quantity, availability of goods to be purchase or about the terms and conditions of sale he sends a letter of enquiry to the seller. Letters of enquiry may roughly be put into the following categories:

(a) An enquiry made at the buyer's own initiative.
(b) An enquiry made in response to the seller's offer or advertisement
(c) A routine enquiry made by an old buyer in the usual course of business
(d) An enquiry for some favour like some special price, relaxation of terms and conditions etc.

A letter of enquiry is ideally a direct approach letter. It should, therefore, be straightforward, courteous and to the point. Special care must be taken about the opening that sets the tone of urgency or the need for information and the close of the letter that shows the writer's expectation of a quick response.

5.1.2 Types of Letters of Enquiry

Letters of enquiry can broadly be divided in to two basic types

(a) Letters of enquiry asking for favour of information regarding goods, services, strategies or personnel without the intention to make an immediate purchase. Such information is usually required for planning trade or individual purchases.
(b) Letters of enquiry linked to the possibility of purchases based on the information provided by the seller in his reply. These letters are further classified as:
- **Solicited letters of enquiry:** A solicited enquiry is a letter written after seeing an advertisement or offer in a newspaper or magazine, television, hoarding, handbill, etc. It is usually a brief letter, which mentions the medium in which the advertisement was observed.
- **Unsolicited letters of enquiry:** An unsolicited enquiry is a letter written by a prospective buyer, at his own initiative asking for information regarding the price, quality, capacity, power, fuel or power consumption, warranty/guaranty period, discounts, rebates, etc. The enquiry is known as an unsolicited enquiry, because it has been the result of the prospective buyer's own desire. The seller has not initiated it.

5.1.3 Drafting of Enquiry Letter

1. **Purpose of Letter:** While drafting an enquiry letter, one must mention the purpose whether he/she needs goods, services or information.
2. **Request for Details:** While making an enquiry, one must request for the details of the goods or services such as price-list, catalogue, etc.
3. **Details of Business:** An enquiry letter should mention the details of the business and the reason related to the interest in the goods or services.
4. **Reference:** An enquiry Letter should mention the reference from where they got the information about the seller.
5. **Terms of Purchase:** The terms and conditions related to the goods and services like credit, discount, packaging, mode of delivery, etc.
6. **Bulk order:** Enquiry letter should include an idea about the quantity needed by the purchaser so that he can avail best possible price as well as rebate in cash price.

5.1.4 Replies

All enquiries must be replied promptly. Delay in replying a letter of enquiry would prove counterproductive as it would convey a poor image of the seller.

When a reply is sent, make sure it includes all the information that has been asked for such as prices, terms of sales including discounts, credit delivery, etc. Include with the letter the price list or the catalogue or this can be sent separately too.

All replies to 'first' enquiries, whether made at the buyer's own initiative or in response to the seller's offer/advertisement must be so carefully drafted that an order is ensured. Remember the letter should only have positive information which is elaborated as the selling points so that the order is given. The letter should in all means try and replace a salesman and must convince the buyer about the favourable terms and conditions, the after sales service and the most important being the quality of the product.

The following letters illustrate these points.

1. **Enquiry Letter**

10th July

Dear Sir,

During a recent Trade fair held here, I saw some samples of your new granite tiles for flooring. I would like to make use of them for the interiors I am designing for a new housing complex. Please give me the following information:

(1) In what sizes, colours and designs can you supply the tiles?
(2) Are the tiles likely to be affected by moisture?
(3) Is any special processing of the under-flooring required?

I shall be most grateful if you could reply me with answers to these questions by Friday, the 17th July

Yours faithfully,
XYZ

2. Enquiry Letter

10 May

Dear Sir,

We are opening a new school at New Panel, with 36 classrooms and will be buying a large number of desks and chairs. We would be pleased to receive your catalogue of moulded plastic school furniture together with your price-list.

The school has to be fully equipped by the end of May, and we will expect supplies to reach us by 15 May.

If you can supply suitable goods, we may place further orders as we will be expanding our schools.

Yours truly,
XYZ

Reply to Enquiry

Dear Sir,

Thank you for your enquiry dated 10th July about our new granite titles for flooring. We have enclosed a copy of our catalogue showing the designs and range of colours in which the tiles are available.

M/s. Dhruv & Co, 23 M.G. Road, Secunderabad, is a reliable firm and handles all our products in your area. We have asked Mr. Dhruv to get in touch with you; he will inspect the premises and advise you whether the moisture would give rise to any problem. Our new PVC tiles are durable and, if they are laid according to the instructions provided by us, will give you lasting satisfaction.

Yours faithfully,
XYZ

Reply to Enquiry

Dear Sir,

In reply to your enquiry, we are happy to send you our catalogue and price-list of moulded plastic chairs and desks. They are enclosed herewith.

You will find models shown on page 3-4 particularly suitable for schools. They are available in several sizes, so as to be suitable for children of different age groups. We have supplied these chairs and desks to many schools, both in Hyderabad and nearby areas.

The schools have found them highly satisfactory as they require very little maintenance and are easy to clean. Their pleasant appearance adds to the attractiveness of the classroom. The variety of colours in which they are available gives you an added advantage.

We shall be very happy to discuss your requirements personally. Please call us at any of the numbers given above for an appointment for our representative to meet you.

Yours truly,
XYZ

5.1.5 Sample Letter

Example 1: Write a letter of enquiry to a manufacturer of batteries seeking information about the different kinds of product so that a decision may be taken for placing an order.

Dear Sir,

We are interested in buying Electrochem Lithium Batteries about which we recently read in the reputed journal 'Science Reporter'.

Please be kind enough to send us the latest information about your product so as to help us take a decision in this regard.

Yours faithfully,

Manager
(Technical)

5.2 Orders and Replies

Enquiries and replies to enquiries lead to orders and their fulfillment, thus continuing the chain of two-way communication. A buyer seeks information regarding the product/ services of his need, and it is the seller's effort to make the best possible offer. In fact the offer made in the reply is supposed to be attractive enough to secure an order from the buyer. An order may also be placed without an enquiry if the buyer already knows about the product, manufacturer, the seller/supplier, through a catalogue, advertisement, etc.

Letters related to ordering of goods are central to a company's business; all other letters arise from orders for goods and services.

Orders are routine letters and their effectiveness depends on the accuracy of the details. Most of the contents of an order can be tabulated.

Replies to order are treated as opportunities to build up goodwill and relationship with new customers, uncertain customers, regained customers as well as long standing loyal customers. Interest in replying to orders goes a long way in creating goodwill.

5.2.1 Orders

Before placing an order, get all the details of what you want to buy. Group the details under the following headings.

Product, its specifications and quality

Give a full and accurate description of the goods you need. Some products come in a variety of sizes, colours etc. Identify the exact product you want by specifications like

(i) Size, (of product or the packing)
(ii) Colour
(iii) Catalogue number
(iv) Model number
(v) Unit price

State the correct quantity required. Different products are sold in different measures; liquids in litres; solids in kilograms, dozens or hundreds; large products like cupboards, in units etc.

Packing

Some products like liquids, grains and tablets, have packing of various quantities; shampoos are packed in 100ml, 200ml, etc.; grains are packed in bags of 1 kg, 2 kg, and so on; tablets come in strips of ten or bottles of 50, 100, etc. some products are available in different types of packing like bottles, tins and sachets. The required packing should be specified in the order. Packing goods suitably for transport is the responsibility of supplier; buyer's instructions are needed only if the goods are to be specially packed for any special purpose.

5.2.2 Drafting an Order

(a) An Order can be placed in a form of a letter clearly stating the following
   (i)   Reference to the seller's letter number, date
   (ii) Catalogue number/price list, price quoted therein.
   (iii) Specification of goods, quantity required.
   (iv) Shipment/ forwarding directions, clearly mentioning whether certain goods are to be sent by parcel post, passenger train, truck, lorry or ship.
   (v)   Instructions regarding packing, insurance etc.
   (vi) The manner of payment agreed upon.
   (vii) Time, limit, discount, quality, etc.

(b) Order form: Many firms now-a-days use "order forms" or "order blanks" for this purpose. These are standardised forms containing all the necessary instructions and blank space for the required details to be filled in at the time of sending out an order. As placing orders is a kind of routine mater, these order forms are quite useful for repeat orders.

It should, however, be emphasised that an order form is invariably sent with a covering letter. So, the covering letter, usually very brief, is also an important letter. It becomes more important if the buyer has to mention any special matter or give any instructions/ information not contained in the order form.

5.2.3 Examples

1. Example of an Order Letter

RAMA STORES
10, Outer Circle, Tokarkhada
Silvassa

7th April, 2013
The Sales Manager
Unique Boutique Products
16, Andheri (West)
Mumbai.

Dear Sir,

Thank you for your catalogue and price list. We are glad to place our first order with you for the following items.

Sr. No.	Product No.	Description	Quantity	Unit Price ₹	Amount ₹
1	1000	Anti-wrinkle cream 50 gms.	500 pcs.	10	50,000
2	6056	Moisturizer 100ml.	500 pcs.	75	37,500
3	4356	Almond cold cream	500 pcs.	85	42,500
4	5478	Under eye gel 500 gms.	500 pcs.	110	55,000
5	3078	Shampoo Normal hair 200 ml.	500 pcs.	75	35,000
					2,20,000

Since we require the above items to replenish our exhausted stock, we request you to kindly dispatch them by passenger train. We shall arrange for taking delivery of the goods at our end.

The R/R and the invoice, at 7% discount may please be sent through Bank of Baroda, Vapi

Yours faithfully,
XYZ

2. **Example of Order Letter:** On behalf of Rama Stores write a letter of order to the local wholesale supplier for certain specified items that you have already ordered on telephone.

RAMA STORES
10, Outer Circle, Tokarkhada
Silvassa

9th April, 2013
The Sales Manager
Smart Suppliers,
10, Dapada Road,
Silvassa
D. & N.H.

Dear Sir,
    Further to our order given on telephone yesterday I am enclosing herewith our order No. Rs/54/23 for immediate supply of the items as specified.
    As the goods are urgently required. I request you to kindly get them delivered to us within 3 days.

Yours faithfully,
Encl: Our Order.

```
ORDER FORM
                            RAMA STORES
                      10, Outer Circle, Tokarkhada
                                Silvassa
No. RS/54/23

To,
The Manager
Smart Suppliers,
10, Dapada Road,
Silvassa,
D. & N.H.

Dear Sir,
    Kindly supply the following:
```

Sr. No.	Product No.	Description	Quantity	Unit Price ₹	Amount ₹
1	C/34	Ladies' hair brush	200	50	10,000
2	C/35	Ladies' Hair Comb	200	20	4,000
3	O/35	Facial Tissue	100	40	4,000
				Total	18000
				Discount 15%	2700
				Net	15300

Please send delivery note in duplicate
Yours faithfully,
XYZ

5.2.4 Fulfilling Orders

An order must be promptly acknowledged in either of the following ways:
   (a) By writing a special letter of acknowledgement
   (b) By filling in a printed acknowledgement card and posting it immediately on receipt of the order.

   The acknowledgement of an order should have following aims;
   (a) Building up goodwill by expressing gratitude for the customer's interest in the seller.
   (b) Legal acceptance of all the points mentioned in the order.
   (c) Reference to the date of receipt of the order.
   (d) Statement of when the order will be fulfilled and when it will be delivered.
   (e) Statement of desire to be of further service to the customer.

Given below is a sample order acknowledgement card:

```
                    UNIQUE BIOTIQUE PRODUCTS
                         16, Andheri (West)
                              Mumbai
No._____              Date: _____


    Thank you for your order letter No. ................... dated.................
    The goods ordered by you will be dispatched within ...........
    We appreciate your cooperation.
For GEN. MANAGER
(Sales)
```

The receiver's address is typed/printed on the other side of the card.

Sample order acknowledgement letter

```
                    UNIQUE BIOTIQUE PRODUCTS
                         16, Andheri (West)
                              Mumbai
No._____              Date: _____


Rama Stores
16, Outer Circle
Tokarkhada, Silvassa.


Dear Sir,

    Thank you very much for you order letter No.......... dated_____ April 2013.

    We are arranging to send the goods ordered by you within fifteen days by passenger train. We are sure you will be fully satisfied with the goods. At this price they represent the best value for your money.

    Besides these, we manufacture and supply a vast range of herbal and natural health-care items. We are enclosing herewith our latest catalogue which you may be interested in ordering.

    We look forward to a satisfactory and cordial working relationship.


Yours faithfully,
XYZ
```

Reply to Example 1

Date: ....
Rama Stores
16, Outer Circle
Tokarkhada,
Silvassa

Dear Sir,

    We are pleased to inform you that your order of 7th April has been promptly fulfilled. The cosmetic items ordered by you have been dispatched and you should be getting them in about ten days from today.

    If you wish to have any further information please do not hesitate to contact us. We shall be happy to serve you in whatever way we can.

Yours faithfully,
XYZ
Encl: Copy of Invoice.

Reply to Example 2

Date: ....
Rama Stores
16, Outer Circle
Tokarkhada
Silvassa

Dear Sir,

    Thank you very much for your interest in us and your order No …… of 9th April.

    As desired by you we are delivering the goods as specified in your order by our own van. We are enclosing the bill with this letter.

    As it is a local order we are bearing the cost of delivery. We are sure you will find the items entirely satisfactory.

    We look forward to further orders and assure you of our best services.

Yours faithfully,
XYZ
Encl:
1) Bill
2) Delivery note

5.3 Credit and Status Enquiries

5.3.1 Meaning

The goods can be sold on cash or credit basis. Credit is a means through which goods can be bought and sold without cash payment. It is found to be useful to the buyers as well as sellers. When goods are sold on cash, no risk is involved. But when goods are sold on credit a great care is required to be taken. The trader should make enquiries regarding the financial standing, trustworthiness, reputation, character, and financial capacity of the party to which credit is to be extended. Such an enquiry is known as a Status Enquiry.

If the credit facility is offered to all the customers without proper enquiry then it will lead to non-recovery of the dues and the trade will have to suffer heavy losses due to bad debts. Such an enquiry is necessary not only because an element of risk is involved but also to know the financial soundness of a customer, his character and his ability to pay dues. The credit department must look in to the following vital information about the customer.

1. **Financial Soundness of the Customer:** It includes the practice of making prompt payments, reputation for fairness and justice, value of customer's assets, the reserves and the ratio between customer's assets and liabilities.
2. **Customer's Character:** It includes honesty, reliability, trustworthiness and moral conduct.
3. **Environmental condition:** The condition of the customer's business in particular (Internal business environment) and the external environmental conditions affect the individual business.

5.3.2 Sources of Status Enquiry

The trader/supplier can obtain information about the status of a customer through different sources which must be reliable. Generally, the following sources are available:

1. **Trade Reference:** Generally, a new customer asking for a credit facility has to give name and address of at least two persons or firms to whom enquiry about the customer's financial position may be made. In such cases, the seller has to obtain necessary information from those persons and after receiving a satisfactory report from the referees the order has to be executed. But in this case precaution should be taken to avoid the possibility of frauds and to see that the referees are reliable and trustworthy. It may happen that a person or the group may demand a credit facility and give references of two persons belonging to the same group who will provide favourable information which may be false.
2. **Bank Reference:** A customer placing an order with a firm for the first time usually gives bank references which contain the name of the bank, location of the bank, type of account number, operating instructions, etc. to prove his creditworthiness in the market. He gives the names of his bankers so that the seller may write to them and

get information about the financial position of the party. After the inspection of the customer's account in the books of the bank it has to supply information about the financial position and creditworthiness of that customer. Sometimes the bank may not give the details of its client to an individual as the accounts are to be kept confidential. In such case, the customer himself will have to request to his banker to provide this information to the trade.

3. **Trade Associations:** Trade Association is the association of persons related to the trade and industry. They maintain the basic information about their members. A businessman can obtain necessary information about the solvency of the members from trade association.
4. **Credit Enquiry Agencies:** The agencies collect information regarding the financial position of local traders. For a fixed annual subscription or a fixed charge for each enquiry, information can be obtained from them about the financial standing and creditworthiness of the firm with whom the enquiry wants to establish business relations.
5. **Government Reports:** Sometimes the Government will publish financial reports of certain companies in their Official Gazettes and Commercial Magazines. The suppliers can obtain useful information from this source.
6. **Financial Statements:** On the basis of trading, profit and loss account, balance sheet for the last 5-10 years a real conclusion about the financial soundness of the company can be drawn and decision about granting of credit can be easily taken.

It should be remembered that the ultimate responsibility of granting credit rests with the trader/supplier himself. The bankers are also providing useful information without any obligation.

5.3.3 Drafting Letters for Trade and Bank References

A new customer asking for a credit facility does not supply the trade references, and then a businessman has to ask for the trade references and bank references. This letter has to be written very carefully because there is a possibility of cancellation of the order itself if the pride of the customer is hurt. Generally, this letter contains the following aspects:

1. Give the reference of the original order.
2. Thank the customer (the party) for placing the order for goods.
3. Request the customer to give a trade reference or bank reference. While making this request the businessman/trader has to state that asking for a trade reference from a new customer is a routine matter and convention followed by the firm.
4. Request the customer to supply the information as early as possible to enable him to execute the order immediately.
5. To extend the co-operation and readiness to reform the favour demanded.
6. The amount of transaction and the period of credit. This would help the referee to understand the risk involved in giving credit
7. A stamped and self-addressed envelope may be enclosed for the use of the reference and prompt reply.

5.3.4 Specimen Letters

Example 1: Hena Traders Ltd. has received a first order from a firm not known to them. They are writing a reply to the firm.

HENA TRADERS LTD.
11, ADIVASI BHAVAN, SILVASSA

Dear Sir,

    We are very much obliged to receive your order of 22nd March, 2014.

    As this is our first transaction with you, we request you to furnish us with the name of your banker as a reference and a couple of other trade references. We always follow this practice in dealing with new customers.

    We shall make preparations to execute your order when you will complete above formalities.

    We hope this to be the beginning of a long and cordial relationship between our firms.

Thanking you,

Yours Faithfully,

Sandeep Shah
(Partner)
For Hena Traders

Example 2: Letter asking for credit and giving references.

M/s MODI BROTHERS
786, Mount Merry Road, Mumbai

To,
Hena Traders
Shop No. 11, Adivasi Bhavan,
Silvassa,
D. & N. H.

Dear Sir,

    We thank you for your prompt reply to our letter. We appreciate the need for references; we are giving below two names and addresses of reputed firms with whom we have been dealing for more than fifteen years.

1. Nalini Departmental Stores
   151, M.G. Road, PUNE - 411 001.

2. Kunjal Trading Company,
   172/6, Canada Corner, NASHIK

Our bankers are State Bank of India, Bank Road, Mumbai. Please write to us if any additional information is required. We also propose to purchase goods worth ₹ 10,000 from your firm on the basis of three months credit facility.

We shall appreciate an early intimation of your decision concerning this order.

Yours Faithfully,

SUBHASH MODI

Example 3: A potential buyer had suggested his bankers name for information as to his financial position. Draft a suitable letter taking up the reference.

M/s SEEMA CREATION COMPANY
CONFIDENTIAL

2nd, Floor, Imperial Theater Bldg.,
Dr. Dandekar Marg,
MUMBAI - 400 004.
2nd November, 20.....

The Branch Manager,
State Bank of India,
Bank Road,
MUMBAI

Dear Sir

Ref: Credit Information of C.K. and Co. Ltd.

M/s C.K. and Co. Ltd. has shown interest in purchasing our 'Computer Discs' in order to popularise them in the North. For this purpose they have asked us to give them credit of ₹ 60,000 for three months. Since we have had no business dealing with them earlier, we asked them for trade references. The firm has given your name as trade reference. Since we are dealing with your bank for a long time, we thought of asking you about the financial status of this firm.

Kindly let us know in all confidence whether we should supply 'Computer Discs' worth ₹ 60,000 to his firm on credit.

We assure to you that the information supplied by you will be treated as strictly confidential and you will not have any legal responsibility for the same.

In case you ever need similar information about any firm which we have dealings with, we shall always be prepared to serve you.

We shall await your valuable advice before we take action in this matter.

Yours Truly,

(Arun Gaikwad)
Credit Manager
For M/s SEEMA CREATION COMPANY

5.3.5 Replies to Status Enquiries

The following are some of the principal points which should be considered while drafting replies to status enquiries.
1. **Brief Replies:** The replies to status enquiries should be brief. Only necessary information should be given. Irrelevant details should be avoided.
2. **Tactful Reply:** The referee has to be very tactful. He should give only relevant information which is based on personal knowledge and his experience.
3. **Precaution:** The amount should be mentioned only if the enquiry definitely mentions the amount of credit he proposes to give.
4. **Unfavourable Opinion:** If an unfavourable opinion is to be expressed it should be expressed with tact and caution. In such circumstances the best way is to express inability to say anything about the party.
5. **No Responsibility:** Whether the opinion expressed is favourable or unfavourable, it should be made clear that the matter should be treated as strictly private and confidential. It should be mentioned that the correspondent accepts no responsibility for the information given in the letter.
6. **To Avoid Mentioning the Name of the Firm:** It is advisable that while giving an adverse opinion about a person or a firm, the name of the person or the firm concerned should not be mentioned.
7. **Objectivity:** A care should be taken to be thoroughly on giving opinion. The objective facts must be set out upon clarity and yet diplomatically where it is found that giving one's opinion might damage the business prospects of the firm under reference the party to whom reference is made has every right to refuse to give any opinion.

Replies by the Persons Referred To

The replies sent by the referees can be divided in to three types based on their contents
1. Favourable replies
2. Unfavourable replies
3. Partially unfavourable replies

Contents of a Favourable Reply

This replies express satisfaction with the credit standing of the customer about whom the enquiry has been made. It contains the following
1. A polite reference to the enquiry.
2. A statement mentioning the nature of the customer's credit worthiness.
3. A statement mentioning the financial position and business prospects of the applicant.
4. A statement stating recommendation of the credit asked for.
5. A request to treat the information as confidential.

Contents of an Unfavourable Reply

An unfavourable reply requires to be drafted very carefully so as to avoid any sign of embarrassment or pointing towards the writer's unsatisfactory relations with the credit applicant. The following points should be considered for drafting an unfavourable reply.

1. The phrases 'Strictly Confidential' or 'Private and confidential' should be written between salutation and the first line of the first paragraph of the letter.
2. A reference to the enquiry mentioning how long you have been acquainted with the applicant.
3. A statement that it is not possible to give the required assurance about the firm, which is a subject of the status enquiry.
4. The reason for not able to give the assurance.
5. A request to treat the information as confidential.

Contents of Partially Unfavourable Reply

Partially unfavourable replies should be written tactfully without making any general comment about the financial standing of the credit applicant in question. The following point should be considered for drafting an unfavourable reply.

1. The phrases 'Strictly Confidential' or 'Private and confidential' should be written between salutation and the first line of the first paragraph of the letter.
2. A reference to the enquiry.
3. A statement about the nature of business operations of the subject of the enquiry. For example: Is good but a slow payer; Is very honest but not very capable etc.
4. To mention the applicant's business failures, impoliteness if any.
5. Mentioning the good qualities of the applicant like, his ability to face difficulties etc.
6. An opinion of the extent to which credit can be given.
7. A request to treat the information as confidential

Example 1: Favourable Reply.

LALIT INDUSTRIES LTD.

28th September, 20.....
The Manager,
Mahaveer Textile Agencies,
100, Azad Hind Road,
Fort, Mumbai - 400 023.
Confidential

Dear Sir,
    In response to your letter of 20th September 20....... we have to state that the firm in question has a sound financial position and enjoys a good reputation in the market, and has a turnover of Rupees four lakhs per year. Evidently, there should be no reason to suppose that it is risky to supply them goods on credit to the extent of Rs. 50,000.

This information is given in confidence and the bank shall not accept my legal responsibility.

Yours Faithfully,

Ajit Mane

Manager

For LALIT INDUSTRIES LTD

Example 2: Unfavourable reply.

LALIT INDUSTRIES LTD

28th September, 20.....

The Manager,

Mahaveer Textile Agencies,

100, Azad Hind Road,

Fort, Mumbai - 400 023.

Confidential

Dear Sir,

In response to your letter of 20th September 20....... we have to state that the party in question does not enjoy credit facilities with the bank for the last eight months. It is reported that the bank had considerable difficulty in recovering previous loans and advances from the party due to their adverse financial position.

This information is given in confidence without any prejudice and without any legal responsibility on our part.

Yours Faithfully,

Ajit Mane

(Manager)

For LALIT INDUSTRIES LTD

Example 3: Partially Unfavourable reply.

LALIT INDUSTRIES LTD

28th September, 20.....

The Manager,
Mahaveer Textile Agencies,
100, Azad Hind Road,
Fort, Mumbai - 400 023.

Confidential

Dear Sir,

    In response to your letter of 20th September 20....... we have to state that the party in question is found quite enterprising. We have had business relations with this firm for the last 6 years and the firm has never deferred payments for longer periods, however our experience in the last two years is that the firm has slightly delayed in making payments.

    This information is given in confidence without any prejudice and without any legal responsibility on our part.

Yours Faithfully,

Ajit Mane

(Manager)
For **LALIT INDUSTRIES LTD.**

5.3.6 Informing the Customer

The decision to grant or refuse credit will depend on several things. The financial position and credit limit is an important factor but the particular risk associated with granting of credit cannot be neglected. When the decision is taken about granting or refusing credit, the customer is informed.

5.3.7 Granting Credit

When the credit is granted, it opens the avenues for customary orders. This is a pleasant message to convey and should be written with a note of welcome. The letter gives information about the routine terms of shipment of goods and payment of bills.

Following points should be considered while drafting letter of grant
1. Statement that credit is approved.
2. Information about regular terms.
3. Message of goodwill

Example 1: Following Letter illustrates the suitable tone for granting credit.

DHARMESH TILES PVT. LTD.

Dear Sir,

We are happy to inform you that your application for a credit account has been approved.

Your account has been opened on a monthly basis. You can either pay the bill for each consignment within 10 days of the delivery of goods or take advantage of the 3% cash discount, or you may pay the entire bill amount in the month following your purchase.

We send our monthly bills in the first week of each month, the payment is to be made by the 10th of the month.

We are looking forward to receiving your first order which will mark the beginning of a long and pleasant business relationship.

Yours Faithfully,
ABC

5.3.8 Refusing Credit

Refusing credit is one of the most unpleasant messages among all the negative messages for the writer as well as the reader.

Utmost care should be taken to analyse the situation carefully before conveying the message. If you show personal interest, you have a better chance of persuading the customer to place his order on cash. One must make every effort to win the customer.

It is better to avoid vague reasons for the refusal; it is more useful to discuss it in a friendly way with the customer. Conditions and circumstances do not remain the same; they may change so as to become more favourable to the customer. An offer to reconsider the application at a later date can soften the refusal.

Considering the customer's view point and understanding his needs, the customer should be acquainted with the benefits he can get by buying on cash, like

(a) Saving capital by getting discounts for cash payment.
(b) Ensuring fresh stock by buying in small lots (fashion goods, medicines and technological products become out-dated rapidly).
(c) Lowering expenditure on cash buying and passing on the advantage of low prices to valued customers to build up goodwill.
(d) Freedom from commitments

A positive attitude and approach makes it easier to persuade the customer to buy in small quantities in cash.

Following points should be considered while drafting letter of refusal:

1. Statement that enquiries related to credit are complete
2. Explanation of the strengths and weaknesses of the customer
3. Statement of refusal with apology

4. Suggestions for improvement, advantages of cash buying
5. Inducements to buy on cash and assurance of co-operation
6. Expression of confidence that the customer will understand the situation and place orders on cash.

Example 1: Following Letter illustrates the suitable tone for refusing credit

---

Dear Sir,

We have completed enquiries in connection with your credit application and our understanding of the situation is as follows:

As you are going to open a new shop you will have to face a good deal of competition, and it will take some time for you to build up a sound business. The risks at the initial stage are greater and we feel that it is advisable to avoid commitments at this stage.

As soon as you have established yourself firmly, we shall be glad to reconsider the credit terms. At present, we suggest that you spread your large order in to small cash orders, over a period of five months. This will give you the benefits of discount which we offer on cash purchases. The goods will be delivered promptly when you require them.

We are sure that you will understand why we are refusing your request for credit now, and that you will let us have your instructions for dispatching your first consignment.

Yours Faithfully,
ABC

5.4 Sales Letters

5.4.1 Introduction

Sales Letters are the most important form of business communication. Their primary aim is publicity or to reach out to a large number of people interested in a particular product or service and turn them in to buyers. Sales letter is a letter written by a company mainly for the sale or publicity. Every business has a competitive market and no business can be done successfully without publicity in one or the other form.

A sales letter is defined as *'a letter written for the purpose of effecting or increasing the sale of goods and services'*. In its broader sense each and every letter sent by a businessman may be called as a sales letter, because the ultimate aim of sending a letter is maximising the profits by maximising the sales, e.g. reply to an enquiring is given with the intention of securing the orders.

5.4.2 Characteristics of Sales Letters

1. **Lengthy Communication:** A typical sales letter often runs into two or three pages. The purpose of the letter is to persuade the reader that he needs to buy the product

which the sellers want to sell. The writer has to include in the sales letter all sorts of arguments in favour of the product or service. Almost all sales letters are long letters in contrast with the other business letters that are supposed to be short and precise.
2. **Focus on particular group of customers:** Sales letter is essentially meant for a particular class of consumers. No product or service can be of interest to all kinds of consumers. For example: Certain products are specially designed for children, for women, for body builders etc. A sales letter for any of these products will be sent to the prospective buyer of that product.
3. **Specialised Information:** An effective sales letter discloses sufficient information about the product offered and is always backed by the specialised knowledge about the needs of the consumer. Supplementary literature stating the details of the product, facts and figures comparing the product offered with the rivals in the market is often supplied with the letter. That is why the sales letters are lengthy and sent along with brochures, pamphlets, leaflets, etc.
4. **Arresting Opening:** An effective sales letters should always start with the catchy subject line, an exclamatory slogan, straight question, abstract question or in whatever way the writer chooses to capture the audience. For example:

"Here is good news for you!"
"We have done it"
"Would you be interested in ...?"
"Could you ever imagine....?"

5. **Emotional Vs Rational Appeals:** Sales letter makes a strong appeal to the consumer or receiver of the letter. Appeals refer to the strategy used to present a product or service favourable to the readers. Appeals can be divided in to two categories emotional and rational. Emotional appeal is directed to our senses like taste, smell, and feeling, hearing and seeing. These appeals include strategies to arouse, love, pride, enjoyment etc. Rational appeals are directed towards reason and include persuasive strategies aimed at saving, making money, doing a job more efficiently etc. The writer of a sales letter make carefully plan his approach on the basis of the product, the needs and expectation of the consumer and how best to appeal to their heart or mind.
6. **Highly Conversational Style:** An effective sales letter is generally written in a highly conversational style. It is supposed to replace the salesman in the sense that the writer enters in to a heart-to heart dialogue with the reader. It has a touch of intimacy and genuine interest in the reader's needs.
7. **Urging Action:** The ultimate aim of a sales letter is to make the reader act, and act with a sense of urgency. The appeal of the letter is so powerful that the reader is convinced of (a) quality of the product, (b) genuineness of the seller's interest in him, (c) wisdom of availing himself of the attractive offer and (d) the value of his time and money.

5.4.3 Advantages of Sales Letters

1. **Advantages over Personal Salesmanship:** Sales letters enjoy some definite advantageous over personal salesmanship and other methods of general advertising. It is easy to avoid a salesman but not a sales letter. It can find its way easily and quickly at almost any place.

2. **Warm welcome:** A sales letter is not unwelcome for it does not impose itself and it comes in very quickly. It can wait patiently till the addressee has enough time to go through it.

3. **Economic:** It is the cheapest way for a businessman to advertise.

4. **Particular in appeal:** Unlike general advertisements appearing in newspaper and magazines, a sales letter is more particular in its appeal for it is addressed to a selected class of customers belonging to a particular age group like financial, professional or social groups.

5. **Personal Touch:** It has the advantage of having a personal touch and of being as brief or as long as may be necessary. There are less chances of it not proving its point. It is clear and can compel action immediately.

6. **No Competition:** A general advertisement may fail to attract attention. A sales letter does not suffer from such competition. It gets all the attention because the reader thinks that it is a personal message to him. A postman with a sales letter is more welcome than a salesman with the product. A sales letter gets a direct and free entry into the rooms which says, "*No Admission Without Permission*".

Thus, a sales letter plays quite an important role in conducting business in general and in direct selling.

The preparation of a good sales letter is a very important factor because many companies have about 5 to 10 drafts made, before a final draft is selected as a sales letter. Sales letters are not sent every day and because wherever it is sent it should be written with the following points in mind.

1. The purpose, the writer wishes to achieve.
2. All facts regarding the product.
3. A visual of the reader.
4. Selection of the group which will easily buy the product.
5. Arrangement of the arguments by **AIDA**.
    (a) **Attention** (Introduction of the product).
    (b) **Interest** (Giving information regarding the product).
    (c) **Desire** to possess (less expensive and useful).
    (d) **Action** (Easily available).

5.4.4 Structure of a Sales Letter - The Salutation

Salutation plays a very important role in a sales letter especially when a prospective customer is to be addressed. Normally, when we know whom we are writing to, we use the salutations, like Dear Mr. XYZ or Dear Ms. XYZ. While in a sales letter if it is a consumer item then the use of a salutation is mainly for the lady of the house. In a sales letter the writer has more liberty to change the salutation from the Dear, Madam/Sir to phrases like, 'The lady of the House', or 'The Young Lady who follows modern trends'.

Generally, a sales letter is divided into three parts.

(a) Introductory Paragraph: Opening paragraph of the sales letter is treated as one of the most important parts of the sales letter, because the main purpose of writing this paragraph is to attract the minds of the customers towards the product and to compel them to read the letter completely. In this paragraph, the main subject is to be introduced without giving the unnecessary details. For the purpose of attracting the customers, efforts shall be made to appeal to the self interest of a customer by showing him as to how can he save his money or how he can satisfy his needs by purchasing our products. Some slogan like, "*There is a solution to every problem*" or "*We have the solution to your problem*", may be used to attract the minds of the customers. A well written opening paragraph saves a letter from being thrown into a waste paper basket.

(b) Body of the letter: This part contains the main information or message of the letter. The main purpose of this part is to convince the readers about the superior quality and fair price of the product and to induce him to purchase that particular product. This part shall contain all the necessary details about the products like its description, quality, price, colour, size, taste and special features. Depending upon the subject matter this part may be divided into suitable paragraphs. But care should be taken that it is not very lengthy and serious. After giving the description of the product efforts shall be made to induce the customers to search the goods by making different types of appeals in a sales letter. Various types of appeal may be made like Appeal to the Pride of Possession, Luxury Appeal, Appeal of Fear, Safety Appeal, Appeal to Health, Appeal to Natural Love for Family Members, Appeal to Sympathy, Economic Appeal etc.

(c) Closing Paragraph: The main purpose of the second part is to describe the goods and to induce the customer to purchase the goods producing; this purpose is served in the closing paragraph. The customer shall be induced to act immediately. It must point out the benefits of buying the product, e.g. utility, efficiency, economical and a guarantee if possible. This paragraph shall state briefly and clearly in a positive manner as to what a customer shall do after reading the letter. By presuming that a customer is convinced to possess goods an immediate action to purchase goods is expected from him and in the last paragraph efforts shall be made to secure orders immediately.For this purpose, proper conditions like discount, payment by installment, after sales service, etc. shall be given.

5.4.5 Examples

Sales appeal to health

Attention	Dear Mr. Narayan,
	You don't look at the mirror any more. You don't like what you see there.
Interest	You ache all over and cannot sit or stand for any length of time. Your back is killing you.
Desire	But thanks to our ergonomically designed office furniture you can rid yourself of all this suffering. Not only you but everyone in your office will be more comfortable and what is important, output will go up.
Conviction	Allow us the opportunity to introduce the latest designs and bring your office up to date with international health standards. Our generous exchange offer will ensure a new set of furniture at the most economic rates.
Action	There is no need to suffer in silence. Just complete and return the enclosed card. Our sales representative will get in touch and discuss with you a plan tailor made for your office.
	For any queries feel free to contact us on 2520 6615 anytime between 9:00 a.m. to 9:00 p.m., on all days.
	Yours faithfully

Sales appeal to self-esteem

Attention	Dear Student,
	You feel a misfit in your college. You cannot follow lectures and haven't been able to make new friends?
Interest	Your poor communication skills in English single you out. Your pretty face loses its charm when asked to speak in public.
Conviction Desire	Remember, your communication skills reflect your personality and will determine your future. In a globalised world command over spoken and written English will become your most powerful asset. That is why we are sending you the enclosed brochure "Get it Right." Read it carefully and think of the benefits that will come to you and the confidence you will acquire when your conversation makes you the centre of attraction.
Attention	If you want to improve your English speaking and writing skills, fill in the enclosed form today. A one-time payment of just Rs.199 will bring you the book of instructions, a workbook and three CDs. You may return the books and CDs within 10 days if you are not completely satisfied and we will refund the entire amount to you immediately.
	Yours faithfully

Other Sales Letters
Example 1

PETRO BONUS

September, 6, 2006

Dear Petro Card™ Customer,

 Welcome to a whole new experience of buying fuel. You would be very glad to know that Bharat Petroleum has now introduced a new chain of stores; In & Out™ offering a host of convenience based products and services under one roof.

 The In & Out store is designed for modern day households, offering facilities to carry out errands/ chores like bill payments, laundry, ATM, courier, cyber café, booking movie and other entertainment/event tickets, greeting cards, mobile phone pre-paid cards, flavoured popcorns and quick buys for the house, to name a few.

 We at Bharat Petroleum have forged alliances with the leading brands in the country like Hindustan Lever, ICICI Bank, Standard Chartered Grindlays Bank, UTI Bank, DHL Courier Service, SkyPak drop boxes, Tatanova Internet Service, Gold Flake Expressions Greeting cards, Music world, SAREGAMA India Limited, SkyCell Communications, Indya Tickets, Kodak, Owiky's Coffee, Pepsi and Kwality Walls, to offer their products and services from In & Out stores across different cities with a combination of the above being available in different outlets.

 We shall be glad if you could give us an opportunity to serve you in the In & Out stores too. To welcome you, we are also enclosing a special discount booklet for purchases at these outlets. Please do start using these and experience the convenience of In & Out.

 So, simplify life, make it In & Out.

Yours truly,
Warms regard,

Subhankar Sen
Manager – Retail Strategy

Example 2:

Dear Friend,

I don't mind telling you it's not everyone in your town who is getting a chance to receive this exciting opportunity. You were chosen by our computer to receive the enclosed Gift and Savings Certificate.

These documents are issued for your exclusive use! Please return the enclosed Gift and Saving Certificate with the Gift Stamp within 14 days, and you can claim three Mystery Gifts along with a subscription to Reader's Digest at 38% discount!

Your Mystery Gifts will remain a mystery for now: to reveal them in advance would spoil your surprise! And although they cost us only a few rupees to produce, I can promise you that, like our magazine itself, your gifts are something that every member of your family can enjoy.

If you enjoy good reading, but haven't the time to wade through lengthy books on every subject of interest to you, the Digest is really for you. Each monthly issue is a complete library in itself-bringing you, in brisk, no-nonsense articles, the 'guts' of as many as 20 important topics. You'll find the facts you want, and much more.

A trial – at 38% discount

So a trial – at a 38% reduced price – is what we now suggest, instead of Rs.444 (plus Rs.22 postage & handling), at which the yearly subscription price of the magazine now stands, you need to pay only Rs.275 (plus Rs.22 postage & handling) – a fabulous saving of Rs.169!

You have nothing to lose by saying 'Yes' to our offer. And there is no need to send any money now. It will be sufficient for you to pay the postman when he delivers your package of Mystery Gifts. As soon as we know that you have accepted the VPP, we will start sending you copies of the Reader's Digest, month after month, for one full year.

Simply stick your Gift stamp in the 'Yes' box on the enclosed Certificate, detach and post today. By doing this:

- ❖ You claim the Three Mystery Gifts that are waiting for you now; and
- ❖ You get 12 issues of the world's most popular magazine for only Rs.275 (plus Rs.22 for postage and handling) – a cash saving of 38%.

The enclosed certificate is self-addressed and reply-paid: please don't waste it. If you are not interested in trying the Reader's Digest at this time, please do let us know, so that we can pass on this opportunity to somebody else. But if your answer is 'yes', please post your free gift and savings Certificate within the next 14 days.

And finally, if you are still hesitating between a 'Yes' and 'No'- remember all the things you and your family stand to gain by saying 'Yes' !

Yours sincerely,

For Reader's Digest

5.4.6 Conclusion

A sales letter is a more direct and personalised form of advertising. A well written sales letter is not easy to ignore. All winning sales letters follow the AIDA formula. The design, appearance, and presentation of the sales letter must be kept in mind along with the contents. This will ensure a better response of the reader towards the product.

5.5 Complaints and their Adjustments

5.5.1 Introduction

A customer has a wide choice to purchase goods from different suppliers. After placing the order for the goods, when the customer receives the goods, he examines them in order to find out whether they are as per the order placed by him. If there is any difference, then he has to write a letter of complaint to the supplier. It should be remembered that good companies conduct their business in such a manner that there are no complaints from their customers. But the possibility of the mistakes cannot be avoided and the efficiency of the company is judged in the way it handles complaints. A good company handles complaints tactfully. If complaints are treated promptly, sympathetically and tactfully the reputation of the company / firm improves. The customers become sure that they will get satisfactory services from the firm and proper attention will be given towards their complaints.

If proper attention is not given towards complaints, the company may lose its reputation. Hence, the attitude of the company should be to welcome complaints and it should encourage its customers to make complaints, in case of dissatisfaction. The company should immediately try to redress complaints.

5.5.2 Objectives of Complaint Letters

The complaints are made with a view:
1. **To Express Irritation:** To express irritation at the delay, carelessness or cheating on the part of the supplier.
2. **To Make adjustment and Fix the Problems:** To make a request to the supplier to make adjustments and fix the problems.
3. **To Demand Claims and Replacements:** To make claims and to return the goods and ask for replacements or the refund of the price already paid.

5.5.3 Circumstances on which Complaint Letters are to be sent

When the customer receives the goods, he examines them in order to find out if they are as per the order placed by him. If there is any inconsistency, he is required to write to the supplier and bring it to his notice. The following are the circumstances for writing complaint letters.
1. The goods supplied are of an inferior quality as well as short in quantity.
2. Delay in execution of order.
3. The goods have been damaged due to bad packing.
4. The rude behaviour of the staff in the office or the shop or misbehavior of the supplier.
5. The terms and conditions of the contract have been violated.
6. Goods are charged at higher prices.
7. Mistakes in the invoice.

5.5.4 The Adjustment Letters

When complaints are received from the customers, the adjustment letters should be sent for the settlement of misunderstanding and wrong approaches. If a decision could not be taken immediately about complaint or an adjustment, arrangements could not be possibly arrived at, a brief letter of acknowledgement should be written, expressing regret for the course of the complaint or claim and assuring the customer that an investigation and informing him that his claim is under due consideration.

Following aspects should be considered while drafting adjustment letter.

1. The adjustment letter should assume that the customer is honest in his complaint or claim. Suitably amend the letter of adjustment to the reader and show sincere appreciation of his point of view.
2. Write the letter in a spirit of service and fair treatment.
3. Thank the customer for his letter, and for the opportunity that it gives you to explain your policies or to remedy defects in your goods and services.
4. Take the view that the customer is benefitting you by his constructive criticism.
5. Do not make use of dissatisfaction or tell him that his is the only solitary complaint.
6. Emphasize the positive, constructive side of the adjustment problem.

5.5.5 Tips for Writing an Effective Complaint Letter

1. **Concise Letter catch attention:** The purpose of a complaint letter is that it is read; the reader understands the facts clearly and knows what action is expected of him. In general, the only letters that are read fully and understood are those which are concise, clear and compact. Lengthy letters that ramble or are vague will not be read properly. So, to be read, make your letter concise. Make sure that you state the main point in less than five seconds. Your complaint letter may subsequently take a few more seconds to explain the situation, but first the main point must be understood in a few seconds.
2. **Structure of the Letter:** The purpose of a complaint letter is to persuade the reader to take action. Remember the acronym AIDA – Attention, Interest, Desire, Action. This is the fundamental process of persuasion and applies to letters of complaints too. Structure your letter to include the following:
    - **A heading:** Which identifies the name of product, service, person, location, with code or reference number if applicable and the issue being raised.
    - **Statement of facts:** In simple terms with relevant details indicating what was promised and what was delivered. If there is insufficient justification, the recipient organisation will not commit the investment needed to solve the problem. Hence, make sure you state all relevant facts in an orderly manner. Do not make is sound frivolous.
    - **Action Expected:** State the action you expect – a positive request for the reader to react to.
    - **Soften and be constructive:** As a closing point, mention the reputation of the organisation and previous record of satisfactory association. Even if you are very angry, make a positive, complimentary closing, as the objective is to make the

respondent take positive action and resolution of the issue and not get into a long, battle with him. Constructive letters and suggestions make complaints easier to resolve. Threatening people generally does not produce good results.

- **A friendly complimentary approach:** It encourages the other person to reciprocate. He will want to return your faith, build the relationship, and keep you as a loyal customer. People like those who are helpful, nice and friendly. They would not find it easy to help who are nasty and attacking. This is perhaps the most important rule of all when complaining. Be kind to people and they will be kind to you. Ask for their help and they will help you.
- **Try to see things from the recipient's point of view:** The person reading your letter is just like you, who want to do a good job, be happy, to get through the day without being upset. The error must have occurred inadvertently or due to oversight by someone else, but definitely unintentionally. Hence, showing your anger at him will serve no good. Respect the worth and motives of your reader and make him your friend. You will see the result.
- **Be different, positive and constructive:** The customer service staff will be dealing with a whole lot of negative and critical statements all the time. This can be very depressing. If the situation is complex and involves a lot of expenditure, be as flexible as you can to find a way forward, rather than terminate the relationship. Suppliers in general, work harder for people who are understanding, stay loyal and are prepared to work through difficult situations.
- **An authoritative stance:** This does not mean that your tone should be intimidating or warning, but an authoritative tone which makes the recipient respect you is especially important for serious complaints or one with significant financial implications. A well-thought out professional presentation, good grammar and spelling, clarity and firmness in tone while putting forth your expectations are the characteristics of an authoritative letter of complaint. These help to establish your credibility. The reader will believe that you have a valid point. Blame game does not result in results.
- **Use Humor:** The use of Humor often works wonders if your letter is addressed to a senior person. Senior persons dealing with complaints tend to react on a personal level, rather than at procedural levels. Hence, a good natured humor draws their attention immediately and helps in dissipating the conflict. It creates a friendly, intelligent and cooperative impression.
- **The look of the letter should indicate professionalism:** If you have one, use a letterhead. Otherwise, as in any business letter, type your address, communication details, date, address of the recipient etc. correctly, tidily, with proper line spacing, indents etc. If the letter has been copied to someone else, mention the details. If you have attached other pages giving further details, photocopies of documents, product being returned etc. state so, at the foot of the letter by using the abbreviation 'enc'.
- **While returning a faulty product:** check all the facts properly and understand the terms and conditions of sale as well as the return policy of the supplier. Make sure

you are within the specified policy limits. For certain consumer complaints it is helpful to return the packaging, as it contains all the production records. If in doubt, talk to the customer services department to find out what they actually need you to return.

3. **Follow-up:** Generally, the receipt of a complaint letter will acknowledge the complaint and thank the writer for bringing up the matter. While assuring the writer that he is a valued customer, he would take appropriate action, which will be…
   (a) understand the quality issues raised and the circumstances that led to the supply of inferior quality product or service and take corrective action,
   (b) ignore the complaint if it is trivial and the customer is not of great consequence,
   (c) contained or dispute the position taken by the customer in the complaint letter.

All this may take some time. The writer will wait for a reasonable period of time before sending a follow-up letter referring to the complaint letter. He will reiterate the issue raised in the complaint letter and then set a time limit for the corrective action. This step will be taken only if the writer/ customer is certain that he can take the dispute to a higher level.

5.5.6 Examples

Example 1: Complaint concerning wrong goods.

BOOKS 'n' NOOKS
111 - A, Bhavani Shankar Road, Dadar, Mumbai – 400017.

19th January, 2013

Mr. A. Sardesai,
Manager,
Harrisons & Brothers
3, D.N. Road, Churchgate,
Mumbai – 400001.

Dear Sir,

Sub.: Order No. C-157

On 3rd January, I had ordered 24 copies of 'Digital Fortress' by Dan brown and received the parcel on 18th January.

However, on opening the parcel, I found that it contained 24 copies of the 'Da Vinci Code' by the same author. I cannot keep these books as I have enough stock. I am, therefore, returning the books by parcel for immediate replacement as I have several requests for 'Digital Fortress'.

I hope you will look into the matter and dispatch the books before the end of the month.

Yours faithfully,
Sd/-
Pramod Nair
(Proprietor)

Example 2: Reply to Example 1.

HARRISON & BROTHERS

3, D.N. Road Churchgate, Mumbai – 400001.

Tel.: 2234 4201 / 2234 4291 / 2234 8398

21st January, 2013

Mr. Pramod Nair,

Books 'n Nooks

111 - A, Bhavani Shankar Road, Dadar, Mumbai – 400017.

Dear Mr. Nair,

Sub.: Order No. C-157

We received your letter of 19th January and came to know about the mistake that occurred in handling the above order.

This mistake is entirely ours and we apologies for the same. This occurred as there was less staff during this unusually busy time. Moreover both the books have almost similar front covers.

The correct order has been dispatched as soon as we received your letter along with the bill with the deduction of your return parcel postage.

We apologies for the inconvenience caused and assure you of better service in future.

Yours faithfully,

Sd/-

Anand Sardesai

(Manager– Sales)

Example 3: Complaint concerning quality.

KITCHENWARE

Shop 92, Atur Arcade, Gokhale Cross Road, Pune - 41101

0091-20-2554 1133

3rd February, 2013

M/s. Bright Steels,
49, Karve Road,
Cantonment Area,
Pune – 411001.

Dear Mr. Nair,
Order BA - 386

We have been receiving several complaints from customers about the spoon sets purchased from you. The complaint is that the spoons bend easily and appear to be made of poor quality steel. We have had to refund the purchase price in some cases.

On inspection we found that the spoons are part of the batch supplied against the above order of 21st December, and they do seem to be lighter than the earlier sets purchased. The complaints received are about spoons from the batch mentioned above.

As this is the first time we have had such an experience we are sure there has been some mistake in the order. We hope you will accept the return of the unsold balance spoon sets of 54 and replace them with the spoon sets of the quality we had earlier bought. Please let us know how we should send these sets back.

We look forward to a quick response.

Yours faithfully,
Sd/-
Praveen Joseph
(Manager)

Example 4: Reply to Example 3 (Accepting Complaint).

BRIGHT STEELS
49, Karve Road, Cantonment Area, Pune – 411001.
0091-20-2534 2209
brytsteel.com

9th February, 2013

Mr. Praveen Joseph
Kitchen Ware
92, Atur Arcade,
Gokhale Cross Road,
Pune - 411016.

Dear Mr. Joseph,

Thank you for your letter of 3rd February informing us about the defect in the spoon sets supplied to you against Order BA-386. We are glad that you brought it to our notice.

We have, since checked the spoon sets of the batch mentioned by you and found that they are of poor quality. We are still trying to trace how this has happened. However, we are ready to take back the remaining 54 spoon sets.

Please arrange to send back the unsold spoon sets. We are sending you a new batch of 65 spoon sets to replace the unsold ones. The extra 11 sets are without charge to help you provide free replacement if you receive more complaints.

We regret the inconvenience caused to you.

Yours faithfully,
Sd/-
Sameer Shah
(Manager –Quality Control)

Example 5: Reply to Example 3 (Rejecting complaint).

BRIGHT STEELS

49, Karve Road, Cantonment Area, Pune – 411001.

0091-20-2534 2209

brytsteel.com

9th February, 2013

Mr. Praveen Joseph
Kitchen Ware
92, Atur Arcade,
Gokhale Cross Road,
Pune - 411016.

Dear Mr. Joseph,

We received your letter of 3rd February informing us about problems faced by you regarding Order BA- 386. We sympathise with your problem.

We have been doing business with each other for long and you will agree that you have never had any complaints so far. All our spoons are manufactured at the same factory with the same quality material. They are then sent to the inspection Department where they are scrutinised before being sent to outlets.

It surprises me that a whole batch has been found by you to be of poor quality. From your letter it appears that a small number of spoons escaped this quality scrutiny. Though we regret the inconvenience caused, we cannot take back all the unsold stock from the batch mentioned. It is unlikely that the number of defective spoons will be large. We will, however, replace any spoon set found to be defective and are prepared to allow you a special discount of 5% to compensate for your convenience.

We are sure that you will accept this as a fair and reasonable solution of this matter.

Yours faithfully,
Sd/-
Francis D'cruz
(Manager –Quality Control)

Example 6: Complaint regarding bad packing.

NORONHA BOOK DEPOT

29, A. K. Kidwai Road, Wadala (E), Mumbai – 400013.

Tel.: 2413 2533 / 2413 2588

21st February, 2013

The Manager,
National Book Store
43, Crawford Lane,
Fort, Mumbai – 400002.

Dear Sir,

We received our order F-796 of 16th February today.

It is with regret that we inform you that the 25 sets of 60 books each were very badly packed. The outer wrappings of 11 sets were torn and so the books were soiled at the corners.

This is the second time in three months we have had to complain to you about the same matter. We cannot understand why precautions are not taken inspite of the earlier complaints.

Though all the books are not soiled, we definitely cannot sell the ones that are soiled, at the normal prices. As we propose to sell them at a lower price we suggest that you too make an allowance on the invoice cost. If this is not possible we may have to return all the books for replacement.

We hope you will take more care in the packing of books and look forward to a prompt reply.

Yours faithfully,
Sd/-
James Noronha
(Manager)

Example 7: Reply to Example 6.

NATIONAL BOOK STORE

43, Crawford Lane, Fort, Mumbai – 400002.

Phone: 2312 2312.

27th February, 2013

Mr. James Noronha
Manager
Noronha Book Depot
29, A. K. Kidwai Road,
Wadala (E), Mumbai – 400013.

Dear Mr. Noronha,

Order – F - 796

We received your letter of 21st February and are very sorry to know about the damages to the above order.

The packing department informs that they packed the books well with double paper packing. Under normal circumstances this should have been enough. However, on this occasion there were changes in the delivery vehicles twice and the loading and unloading many times might have led to the tearing of the wrappers.

We apologize for not checking the packaging and assure you that you will not have any reason to complain again.

We realise the need to reduce the selling price for the damaged books and readily agree to the special allowance of 10%. We look forward to more orders.

Yours faithfully,
Sd/-
Jayanti Dave
(Manager)

5.6 Collection Letters

5.6.1 Meaning

It is the responsibility of the customer to ensure that all accounts are promptly paid, especially credit accounts. The supplier who has advanced goods on credit expects punctual payment. Collection letters are sent to customers who have failed to clear their accounts at the right time or by the period mutually agreed upon.

5.6.2 Collection Series

It should not be assumed that the customer who has not paid on time is always at fault. They delay may be due to

(1) not receiving statement of account
(2) having overlooked statement of account or date
(3) not being in station
(4) lean season
(5) illness
(6) cheque sent but lost in transit
(7) payment not recorded by supplier
(8) insufficient cash flow or any other unforeseen problem.

At the same time there are customers who are ready to invent excuses and who need to be tackled carefully. Whatever be the cause of delay, collection letters must be polite and tactful. Every customer should be given the opportunity to pay by sending one or two reminders.

Each case must be treated on its own merits – the style and the tone of the letter will depend on the age of the debt, how important the customer is and whether delayed payment is customary. Knowing one's customer helps one to make special allowances in some cases or agree to grant extension of period in some others.

Collection letters are planned in series. The first one might be a gentle reminder giving the statement of account with the amount and due date of payment. Sometimes a printed collection letter with individual details is sent. The customer must be given time to pay before the second collection letter is sent. The second collection letter is sent when there is no response (payment or explanation) to the first. The second letter could politely enquire the reason for non-payment and offer extension of time or payment in installments. It may even enquire if there were any problems regarding goods or invoice. Though polite, the letter should be firm in tone. If the second letter also does not receive any response a third one becomes necessary. This letter must refer to earlier efforts to collect payment and offer a final opportunity to pay by stating a deadline date. It should also state that the supplier has been fair and reasonable but will be forced to take strict action if the third request is ignored.

The supplier must remember that nothing can be achieved by strong and aggressive words. Co-operation from the customer is required not his ill-will. Courtesy and tact is required in handling difficult customers. One may appeal to the customer's sense of fairness, his self-interest or even sympathy. Only when every other plan fails, should one appeal to fear and the threat of legal action.

In most cases the first collection letter brings in response in the form of payment or explanation for delay or request for extension of period or surprise at being reminded as the cheque had already been sent. The supplier may thank for the payment, accept or reject request for extension or apologies for reminding about payment that is already made. If the supplier rejects a customer's request for extension, the latter may pay the outstanding amount with difficulty and take his business elsewhere. If the circumstances and the customer are suitable the supplier can earn the goodwill of the customer by allowing him an extension.

Handling difficult customers needs diplomacy and tact. In some cases it might be better to accept part payment rather than resort to legal action or lose the whole amount. The main thing to keep in mind is that however unpleasant the situation is, the supplier must remain polite.

5.6.3 Examples

Example 1: First Collection Letter to a Regular Customer.

COMFO LUGGAGE
385, S.V.P Road, Girgaum Mumbai
Mumbai – 400005.
Ph. : 23114463 / 2322 3649

3rd March, 2013

Mr. Ajit Pillai,
Manager,
Bags and Baggage,
P.K. ROAD, Near Kalidas Hall,
Mulund, Mumbai - 400096

Dear Mr. Pillai,

Sub: Invoice No. S 169

This is to remind you that you have not settled our invoice No. S 169 for ₹ 62,000 which was due on 15th February.

As you are our regular customer and quite prompt in clearing your payments we are sure that non-payment may be due to some oversight.

We are enclosing a copy of the invoice and request you to send us the cheque as soon as possible.

Yours faithfully,

Mohan Verma

Example 2: Second Collection Letter to a regular customer.

COMFO LUGGAGE
385, S.V.P Road, Girgaum Mumbai
Mumbai – 400005.
Ph. : 23114463 / 2322 3649

25th March 2013

Mr. Ajit Pillai,
Manager,
Bags and Baggage,
P.K. ROAD, Near Kalidas Hall,
Mulund, Mumbai - 400096

Dear Mr. Pillai,

Sub: Invoice No. S 169

   We had written to you on 3rd March reminding you about the above invoice for ₹ 62,000/- which still remains outstanding.

   During our long standing business relationship we have never had to remind you about settling payments. Your silence surprises us. We would be obliged if you would send us an explanation and allow us to be of service to you. If there is a problem we could work out an extension of payment time or an installment system.

We await your remittance to clear the account or an explanatory reply.

Yours faithfully,

Mohan Verma

Example 3: Third Collection Letter to a regular customer.

COMFO LUGGAGE
385, S.V.P Road, Girgaum Mumbai
Mumbai – 400005.
Ph. : 23114463 / 2322 3649

16th April, 2013

Mr. Ajit Pillai,
Manager,
Bags and Baggage,
P.K. ROAD, Near Kalidas Hall,
Mulund, Mumbai - 400096

Dear Mr. Pillai,

We are surprised not to hear from you inspite of sending you two letters dated 3rd March and 25th March reminding you about your outstanding sum of ₹ 62,000. The payment was due in February. We had hoped that you would at least send us an explanation.

Our relations in the past have always been cordial. However, we find it difficult to allow the amount to remain unpaid indefinitely. We regret to say that, under these circumstances, we will have to resort to legal action if there is no response from you by the end of this month.

Yours faithfully,

Mohan Verma

5.7 Circular Letters

5.7.1 Meaning

A circular is a communication meant to notify or convey to all customers, business friends, share holders and employees, certain fundamental changes or important information.

A circular is a letter which contains common information about the business which is printed in sufficient number of copies and which is sent to all the persons related to the business directly or indirectly. Generally, whenever there is any change in the business or its organisation, constitution and management then such a change must be notified to all the customers, suppliers and government officials. In fact, the change is made for the benefits of the businessman himself and to maximise the profits but while drafting the circular letters it is to be stated that the change is made in the interest of customers and to provide better services.

As the same circular is sent to a number of persons care must be taken to see that it contains complete and correct information and can obtain co-operation from the customers. A well drafted circular is highly beneficial to the business as it can obtain co-operation from the customers but at the same time if the wrong information is supplied or the change is notified in the wrong manner or a rude language is used whereby the customers may get hurt and insulted, then it will be very much harmful to the business. As the circular letters are sent to hundreds of persons at a time it may please all of them, or it may hurt many persons at a time. Therefore, it is said that, "Mass production is the merit as well as defect of a circular letter".

5.7.2 Objectives

The objectives to be borne in mind when writing a circular letter are:

A. To give publicity to be contents of the letter.
B. To provide information to a select demographic segment regarding some transaction (internal or external) of a business establishment.
C. To gain the confidence of the reader.

5.7.3 Occasion for Writing Circular Letters

Depending upon the nature and the size of the business, the businessman has to send circular letters on different events. Generally, the circular letters are sent on the following events.

1. Establishment of a new business: When a new business is started by the existing firm then for the purpose of obtaining the same co-operation from the customers a circular is to be drafted. This Circular shall contain the following information.

    (a) Name and address of the new business.
    (b) Nature of the business.
    (c) State of its establishment.
    (d) Qualification and efficiency of the person in charge.
    (e) Quality of the goods offered.
    (f) Any discount or concessions.
    (g) Making an appeal to give a trial order.

2. Opening the New Department: Generally, whenever, the new items or services are offered to the customers, these events have a greater advertising value and the businessman shall obtain the maximum benefits out of such changes. When a new department is started then a circular is to be drafted which contains the nature of a new department, quality of the goods offered opening, date of the department, departmental head, etc. It shall be stated that the new department will maintain the policy of the firm of selling the best products at the competitive prices.

3. Expansion of Business or Change in Premises: On such events a circular is drafted stating that the premise has been changed to offer better services to the customer. In case of expansion, it should be stated, that the expansion of business is possible only due to the co-operation of the customers.

4. Opening a New Branch: When a new branch is opened, the address of the new branch, its opening date, name, qualification and experience of the branch manager, and the quality of the goods shall be stated in the circular letter. It should be argued that the new branch is opened to come nearer to the customers.

5. Admission of Partner: When a new partner is admitted into a business a circular letter is sent to all the customers. Such a circular contains the name, address and the qualification of a new partner and capital brought in by him. An assurance may be given that, due to the admission of a new partner, the firm will be able to render better services to the customers and may supply different qualities of the goods.

6. Obtaining an Agency: When a businessman obtains the agency of a product for a particular area, then he has to advertise this matter by sending the circular letters to the prospective buyers. Such a circular letter contains information about the quality of the product, area and period of agency. An appeal has to be made to the customer to place an immediate order.

7. Clearance Sale: When the stock of a business is to be cleared, i.e. to be sold at concessional rates, then the businessman may announce a clearance sale. In case of a public sale, which is open to all, an advertisement may be given in the newspapers, but when the sale is limited to the regular customers, only then the circulars are sent to them. Such a circular contains information related to the quality and quantity of the goods, opening and closing dates, rate of discount, etc.

8. Sale of a business: When the business is sold out to the third party or when it is closed, then this fact is to be informed to all the customers. Such a circular contains the reasons under which the business is sold out or closed. At the same time, proper thanks shall be given to the customers for giving their co-operation during the previous years.

5.7.4 Drafting Circular Letters for Various Purpose

1. **The Purchase of An Existing Business**
    - ✓ The name under which it will be conducted by the new owner.
    - ✓ A reference to the previous owner if the business was successful in the past.
    - ✓ A reference to the goods and prices which are offered by the new management.
    - ✓ A reference to the comfortable financial position of the new management.

2. **The Establishment Of A New Business**
   - ✓ The name under which it will be conducted.
   - ✓ The date of opening.
   - ✓ A reference to the goods and prices which are offered.
   - ✓ A reference to the comfortable financial position of the management.
   - ✓ A request for a trial order.
   - ✓ An assurance that the firm will provide high quality goods and efficient service.
3. **The Obtaining of An Agency**
   - ✓ The particulars of the agency.
   - ✓ A reference to the product.
   - ✓ A reference to the fact that trade has commenced.
   - ✓ An assurance that the agency will provide high quality goods and efficient service.
4. **Change in the Address of a Business Establishment**
   - ✓ The New address.
   - ✓ The reasons for the shift.
   - ✓ The advantages of the new premises.
   - ✓ A statement about more efficient service in the new premises.
5. **The Admission of a Partner**
   - ✓ The name of the person admitted.
   - ✓ What led to his/her admission?
   - ✓ His/her business background.
   - ✓ A reference to the impact of the new partner on the efficiency of the firm.
   - ✓ A request of customers to continue their patronage.
6. **The Retirement or Death of Partners**
   - ✓ The announcement of the partner's retirement or death.
   - ✓ An expression of appreciation or regret, respectively.
   - ✓ An assurance that business will continue as in the past.
   - ✓ A reference that the finances of the company has been made up with contributions by the remaining partners.
7. **Clearance Sales And Price Reductions**
   - ✓ A polite opening introducing the purpose of the letter.
   - ✓ The name of the establishment.
   - ✓ A detailed description of the products for which the offer is valid.
   - ✓ The reason for the price reduction/ clearance sale.
   - ✓ The period for which the offer is valid.
8. **Introduction of New Products**
   - ✓ A polite opening introducing the purpose of the letter.
   - ✓ The name of the establishment.
   - ✓ A detailed description of the product(s) being introduced.
   - ✓ A reference to whether the product is imported or manufactured locally.
   - ✓ The advantages of buying the product(s).

9. Change in the Constitution of A Firm

- ✓ A polite opening introducing the purpose of the letter.
- ✓ The name of the establishment.
- ✓ A detailed description of the change being introduced.
- ✓ The reason for the change.
- ✓ An assurance that the same efficient service will be available and request for orders.

5.7.5 Examples of Circular Letters

Example 1: Sample Circular Letter Announcing the Purchase of an Existing Business

BEAUTY COSMETICS LTD.

Telephone : 033-262163771	102, Park Villa Road
Telegrams : BEAUTY	Siraj Marg, Kolkata 700 040

3rd December 2013

Dear Sir,

I am happy to announce to you that with effect from the forenoon of 1 December 2013, I have acquired the sole interest in M/s. Beauty Cosmetics Ltd., the manufacturers of several popular cosmetics.

I am retaining the same trade name viz., Beauty Cosmetics Ltd; and continue to operate from the same premises as can be seen in this letterhead. I assure you that the firm will continue the previous policy of sincere, customer friendly service.

Permit me to say that I have introduced additional capital and have already acquired the rights to manufacturers some new products from foreign manufacturers. These will be available in the second hair of January 2014. Please continue the patronage that you gave this firm in the past.

Yours faithfully,

Sonal Sen K.

Example 2: Sample Circular Letter Announcing the Establishment of a New Business.

STUDENT'S BOOK CENTRE
(RETAILERS OF EDUCATON BOOKS)

Phone : 0422 - 2433221   No. 102, D. B. Road, R.S. Puram
Grams : STUDENTS'   Coimbatore 641 002

20th September 2013

Dear Sir/ Madam,

We are happy to announce that we are inaugurating our new, retail, bookshop, viz., students' Book Centre at the address given on this letterhead on 1st October 2013. We invite you most cordially to attend the inauguration of our shop by the General Manager, Channel Paper Mills.

We stock a large variety of paper in a wide range of qualities and prices. We also stock a large spectrum of notebooks, files, pouches, pens and other writing materials. Our firm has a sound financial base and as our name suggests, has been situated at a place from which it can serve the student community in many schools and colleges of that area.

We earnestly request the students, parents, teachers and management of educational institutions in this area to patronise us. We assure our customers of efficient service and high quality products at competitive rates. Do send us a trial order please.

Yours faithfully,

STUDENTS' BOOK CENTRE
C. K. Vijay
Proprietor

Example 3: Sample Circular Letter Announcing the Obtaining of an Agency.

ARUNA GENERAL STORES
(Wholesalers & Retailers)

Phone : 020-65420555   222, College Main Road
Telegrams : ARUNGEE   Pune 2

15th September 2013

Dear Sir,

Iosmetic Products of M/s. Beauty Cosmetics Ltd., 102, Park Villa Road, Siraj Marg, Kolkata 40, for the whole of Siraj Marg and have begun dealing in them.

'Beauty' cosmetics are well known and popular all over India and as you are already aware, our firm is popular with the local public and caters to people from various income groups.

We are already supplying & number of products on a trade basis to retailers in and around Siraj Marg. We are now happy that we can add 'Beauty' products to them. We have enclosed a price list, which will clearly show that all the prices carry a generous discount.

Yours faithfully,
Lakshmi Kiran
(Mrs.) Lakshmi Kiran
Managing Proprietor

Example 4: Sample Circular Letter Announcing a Change in the Address of a Business Establishment.

BEAUTY COSMETICS LTD.

Telephone : 033-262163771   102, Park Villa Road
Telegrams : BEAUTY   Siraj Marg, Kolkata 700 040

3rd December 2013

Dear Sir,

The rapid growth of our business has made it necessary for us to move into larger, more convenient and easily accessible premises. We are happy to announce that from 2 January 2014, our head office will be functioning at: 12, Second Avenue, Tagore Lane Kolkata 700040.

The new premise is on the second floor of 'Modern Mansions'. It is easily accessible, as there is a lift in the building. 'Modern Mansions' also has a car park in the basement. The entire office is air conditioned, creating an ambience conducive to business and work.

We take this opportunity to thank you for your sustained interest in our firm and assure you that the new ambience will aid our business transactions to be performed with greater efficiency.

Yours faithfully,
FOR BEAUTY COSMETICS LTD.
Mrithyunjay K.
Managing Partner

Example 5: Sample Circular Letter Announcing the Admission of a Partner.

KOVAI TEXTILES (P) LTD.

Telephone : 0422-2433765   Civil Aerodrome Post
Telegrams : 'KOVAITEX'   Coimbatore 641 014

1st June 2013

Dear Sir,

We thank you for your continuing patronage. With support from our clients like you our business has been expanding rapidly. We are now happy to inform you that we have inducted Mr. Joseph D'Silva as a partner in our business today.

We are sure that our new partner's long experience as Managing Director of Texotex Mills until his retirement last year will aid us to serve our clients better in a number of areas in our business. Please continue to favour us with your orders as in the past.

Yours faithfully,

KOVAI TEXTILES (P) LTD.
A. J. Reynolds
Managing Partner

Example 6: Sample Circular Letter Announcing the Retirement of Death of Partner.

KOVAI TEXTILES (P) LTD.

Telephone : 0422-2433765 Civil Aerodrome Post
Telegrams : 'KOVAITEX' Coimbatore 641 014

1st June 2013

Dear Sir,

We regret to inform you that Mr. C.S. Sheppard our respected and valued partner, who has been with us from the inception of this company, has decided to retire as a result of ill health. He was closely and actively connected with the growth and development of this firm and we are sorry that he has to leave us.

However, we assure you that the admission of a new, partner Mr. Joseph D' Silva and the induction of his contribution have compensated the withdrawal of Mr. Sheppard's capital. As such we assure you that our firm will continue to serve you with its existing standards.

Yours faithfully,
KOVAI TEXTILES (P) LTD.
A. J. Reynolds
Managing Partner

For death of a partner – alter the first paragraph as follows:

Dear Sir,

With deep regret, we inform you that Mr. C. S. Sheppard our respected and valued partner, who has been with us from the inception of this company *died last week*. He was closely and actively connected with the growth and development of this firm and *we will miss his inspiring presence greatly*.

The words in italics represent the changes. There is no change in the rest of the letter.

Example 7: Sample Circular Letter Announcing Clearance Sales and Price Reductions.

REGAL READYMADES & TEXTILES

Telephone : 0821-2443311   10, Town Hall Road
Telegrams : 'REGALIA"   Mysore 570 001

15th October 2013

Dear Sir,

It has been the policy of our firm for several years to have a clearance sale before the Ramzan - Deepavali - Christmas - seasons to make room for the new stocks for those festival seasons. This year too we shall have a clearance sale for five days commencing from the 21st of this month.

We have enclosed a price list showing the original price as well as the reduced ones. The reductions range from 30 per cent to 45 percent. As our clearance sales have attracted large crowds of customers in the past, we request you to pay us an early visit and we assure you that your visit will be of benefit to you.

Yours faithfully,
REGAL READYMADES & TEXTILES
M. Shivappa
Proprietor

Example 8: Sample Circular Letter Announcing the Introduction of New Products.

Beauty Cosmetics Ltd.

Telephone : 033-262163771   102, Park Villa Road
Telegrams : Beauty   Siraj Marg, Kolkata 700 040

3rd December 2013

Dear Sir,

We have great pleasure in announcing that we have introduced two new products. They are 'No Pimples Cream' and 'Anti Discoloration Cream'. The two products are aimed at a target segment of women from 14 to 40 years of age.

However, you are aware that the problems caused by pimples as well as discoloration are not restricted to women alone but extends to boys and young men. We therefore expect the two new products to be very well received by the public. The introduction is very well complemented by ISI certification of our products as safe, effective, herbal creams. We have also arranged for an advertising campaign to back up the launch of the products.

We earnestly request you to send us your order and give the two products the maximum exposure among your customers at your outlet.

Yours faithfully,
FOR BEAUTY COSMETICS LTD.
Mrithyunjay K.
Managing Partner

Example 9: Sample Circular Letter Announcing a Change in the Constitution of the Firm.

KOVAI TEXTILES

Telephone : 0422-2433765   Civil Aerodrome Post
Telegrams : 'KOVAITEX'   Coimbatore 641 014

1st June 2013

Dear Sir,

We thank you for your continuing patronage with support from our clients like you our business has been expanding rapidly. However, as you are aware, expanding business is linked with need for more funds. We too needed more capital to support our expanding business.

We are happy to announce that to facilitate investment to meet this need for capital; we have converted our firm into a private limited company, and inducted new directors, who will invest the needed capital. Our firm will not be known as:

KOVAI TEXTILES (P) LTD.
We assure you that as usual customer satisfaction will be our main consideration in our business. Please extend to us, the same patronage that you have so kindly given us so far.

Yours faithfully,
KOVAI TEXTILES (P) LTD.
A. J. Reynolds
Managing Partner

Points to Remember

- Enquiries generally figure in the first category of letters sent by an organisation or an individual. They are, first and foremost, information seeking letters.
- Letters of enquiry may roughly be put into the following categories:
    (a) An enquiry made at the buyer's own initiative.
    (b) An enquiry made in response to the seller's offer or advertisement
    (c) A routine enquiry made by an old buyer in the usual course of business
    (d) An enquiry for some favour like some special price, relaxation of terms and conditions etc.
- **Drafting of Enquiry Letter**
    1. Purpose of Letter
    2. Request for Details
    3. Details of Business
    4. Reference
    5. Terms of Purchase
    6. Bulk order
- **Orders**

    Before placing an order, get all the details of what you want to buy. Group the details under the following headings.
    - Product, its specifications and quality
    - Packing: An Orders can be placed in a form of a letter clearly stating the following:
        (i) Reference to the seller's letter number, date
        (ii) Catalogue no/price list, price quoted therein.
        (iii) Specification of goods, quantity required.
        (iv) Shipment/ forwarding directions, clearly mentioning whether certain goods are to be sent by parcel post, passenger train, truck, lorry or ship.
        (v) Instructions regarding packing, insurance etc.
        (vi) The manner of payment agreed upon.
        (vii) Time, limit, discount, quality etc

    An order must be promptly acknowledged in either of the following ways:
    (a) by writing a special letter of acknowledgement;
    (b) by filling in a printed acknowledgement card and posting it immediately on receipt of the order.
- The goods can be sold on cash or credit basis. Credit is a means through which goods can be bought and sold without cash payment. When goods are sold on credit a great

care is required to be taken. The trader should make enquiries regarding the financial standing, trustworthiness, reputation, character, and financial capacity of the party to which credit is to be extended. Such an enquiry is known as a Status Enquiry.

- The credit department must look in to the following vital information about the customer.
    1. Financial Soundness of the Customer
    2. Customer's Character
    3. Environmental condition
- **Sources of Status Enquiry are:**
    1. Trade Reference
    2. Bank Reference
    3. Trade associations
    4. Credit enquiry agencies
    5. Government reports
    6. Financial statements
- **Replies to Status Enquiries**
    1. Brief Replies
    2. Tactful Reply
    3. Precaution
    4. Unfavourable opinion
    5. No responsibility
    6. To avoid mentioning the name of the firm
    7. Objectivity
- The replies sent by the referees can be divided in to three types based on their contents:
    1. Favourable replies
    2. Unfavourable replies
    3. Partially unfavourable replies
- Following points should be considered while drafting letter of refusal:
    1. Statement that enquiries related to credit are complete
    2. Explanation of the strengths and weaknesses of the customer
    3. Statement of refusal with apology
    4. Suggestions for improvement, advantages of cash buying
    5. Inducements to buy on cash and assurance of co-operation
    6. Expression of confidence that the customer will understand the situation and place orders on cash.

- Sales letter is a letter written by a company mainly for the sale or publicity. Every business has a competitive market and no business can be done successfully without publicity in one or the other form
- **Characteristics of Sales Letters**
    1. Lengthy Communication
    2. Focus on particular group of customers
    3. Specialised Information
    4. Arresting Opening
    5. Emotional Vs Rational Appeals
    6. Highly conversational style
    7. Urging action
- **Advantages of Sales Letters**
    1. Advantages over Personal Salesmanship
    2. Warm welcome
    3. Economic
    4. Particular in appeal
    5. Personal Touch
    6. No Competition
- **Objectives of Complaint Letters**
    1. To Express Irritation
    2. To Make adjustment and Fix the Problems
    3. To Demand Claims and Replacements
- **Tips for Writing an Effective Complaint Letter**
    1. Concise Letter catch attention
    2. Structure of letter
    3. Follow - up
- Collection letters are sent to customers who have failed to clear their accounts at the right time or by the period mutually agreed upon.
- A circular is a communication meant to notify or convey to all customers, business friends, share holders and employees, certain fundamental changes or important information. A circular is a letter which contains common information about the business which is printed in sufficient number of copies and which is sent to all the persons related to the business directly or indirectly.
- The objectives to be borne in mind when writing a circular letter are:
    A. To give publicity to be contents of the letter.
    B. To provide information to a select demographic segment regarding some transaction (internal or external) of a business establishment.
    C. To gain the confidence of the reader.

- **Occasion for Writing Circular Letters**
    1. Establishment of a new business
    2. Opening the New Department
    3. Expansion of Business or Change in Premises
    4. Opening a New Branch
    5. Admission of Partner
    6. Obtaining an Agency
    7. Clearance Sale
    8. Sale of a business

FREQUENTLY ASKED QUESTIONS FROM UNIVERSITY OF PUNE EXAMINATIONS

1. Draft a letter on behalf of A to Z Matching Centre, Kolhapur to Kalpana Fashion House, Shrigonda (A. Nagar) complaining about the delay in execution of order of Readymade Garments. **[April 2010]**
2. Write a Sales letter on behalf of Das Electronics, Solapur regarding Refrigerator. **[April 2010]**
3. What do you mean by Circular Letter? Explain in detail the causes of Circular Letter. **[April 2010]**
4. You have received an enquiry as to the financial standing of M/s Mehta & Sons, Mumbai. Draft a letter to M/s Shah Brothers, Pune, the enquirer, giving the favourable reply. **[April 2010]**
5. Write reply to enquiry letter from Swastik Rubber Work Ltd., Patil Industrial Estate, Pune to the proprietor Star General Stores, Bajirao Road, Pune about the price and time of delivery of Raincoats, Umbrellas and Gum boots. **[April 2010]**

Chapter ... 6

JOB APPLICATION LETTERS

Contents ...
- 6.1 Introduction
- 6.2 Meaning
- 6.3 Contents of Job Application Letters
- 6.4 Drafting of Job Application Letters
- 6.5 Types of Job Application Letters
- 6.6 Bio-Data/ Resume/ Curriculum Vitae
- 6.7 Examples of Bio-Data, Resume and CV
- • Points to Remember
- • Frequently Asked Questions from University of Pune Examination

Learning Objectives
- To understand the meaning and contents of job application letters
- To learn how to draft a job application letter
- To study the different types of application letters
- To learn to write a bio –data and to study the different examples of resumes.

6.1 Introduction

Job application letters and preparation of resumes are very important among all the written correspondence. Letters of application for employment is undoubtedly very important from the point of view of unemployed persons seeking some jobs. The purpose of job application is to acquire the job and it is this letter which may affect his whole life as he will be judged first by his application. The experienced mind and eye of the businessman will access the character of the applicant from this letter. An application letter gives a brief description of how the applicant came to know about the vacancy, his qualification and why he feels he would be the right person for the job. Application letters vary according to jobs and hence have to be made job or company specific.

6.2 Meaning

An application letter is nothing short of a sales letter, the product being "you" as the applicant tries to sell his services. Hence an application letter is also a kind of sales letter and should follow similar guidelines. An application letter aims at highlighting the applicant's potential and secure an interview, where the candidate can elaborate on his or her usefulness to the organisation. An Application letter has to stand out among hundreds of applications received by the recruiters.

6.3 Contents of Job Application Letters

1. **Name and address of the applicant**

    Generally, the name of an applicant is written at the top of the letter in the right hand corner and starts with the surname of the applicant. Along with the name and address, the date on which the application is written must also be stated.

2. **Name and address of the employer**

    Sometimes, in the advertisement the name and address of the employers is not given. On such occasion the application is addressed to P.O. Box No. If the name and address of the employer is given in the advertisement, then the address should be carefully written, while writing the inside address. The letter may be directed to a proprietary or partner, but in case of a large organisation or Joint Stock Company the application is addressed to the personnel officer or the head of the institution.

3. **Salutation**

    In the application, two different salutations can be used i.e. Dear Sir or Respected Sir. Generally, when the application is written for the higher post or managerial post then the salutation to be used is 'Dear Sir' and when the application is made for any ordinary or common post then the salutation, 'Respected Sir' is used. To whom it is addressed is the first necessity of the application letter.

4. **Introductory Paragraph**

    (a) If the reply is to an advertisement

    (i) The application should state when and where that advertisement appeared e.g. the name and the date of the newspaper.

    (ii) The applicant must give the Post box number and the address if the name of the advertiser is not known.

    (b) If it is an Unsolicited (without advertisement) Application

    The applicant should explain his interest in the kind of work for which he is applying and must begin the introductory paragraph with the following words:

    "Being given to understand that there is a vacancy for the post ....."

    (c) The applicant must state the nature of the position for which the application is made. His position should be underlined in order to remove all ambiguity.

5. **Body of the Letter of Application**

    The application must state honestly, modestly and briefly the following:

    1. **Educational Qualification:** The name of the College or University from which the Applicant has passed.

    2. **Age and Experience: The applicant mentions his date of birth or the age here..** (In case the applicant has left his previous employment) the reasons that are making the applicant decide to leave the present job, if while applying the applicant is employed somewhere.

    3. **General Ability:** The applicant's general ability for performing a work must be mentioned.

    4. **Special Qualifications: An applicant must write his extra qualifications** that may be useful to the employer so that his expertise can be gainfully used in the organisation.

5. **Fitness for the position:** for which the applicant is applying. Here, the applicant must mention only those qualifications in which he or she excels and which the applicant thinks the employer will revalue. No exaggerated claims or show of too much of modesty should be done,
   6. **Terms and Conditions:** The applicant must state the terms and conditions under which he is willing to serve, incase he get appointed.
   7. **Reference:** The applicant must give names of persons or firms to whom references can be made in respect of his character and suitability for the post. (The applicant must take permission from referees before mentioning their name in the application).
6. **Concluding Paragraph**
   1. The applicant must give an assurance that he will work hard and will work with all his capacity and strive to be a good employee.
   2. The applicant must request for an interview in order to discuss personally his terms and conditions. The applicant must never promise anything more than what he can reasonably do.
   3. The applicant must end his letter by leaving a pleasing impression on the mind of the reader

6.4 Drafting of Job Application Letters

1. It should be remembered that the immediate purpose of an application is not to get a job but to get an interview.
2. Do not discuss your family problems in the application.
3. Do not state that you are applying for the job because you are dissatisfied with the present job.
4. Do not talk badly your present employer.
5. Do not give false information.
6. Maintain the "You - attitude" in your application. The application should be written in such a way to convince the employer about the benefits he will get by appointing the applicant.
7. As far as possible avoid the discussion regarding expected salary.
8. Unnecessary details should be avoided.
9. Do not try to get the job by obtaining the sympathy of the employer.
10. (a) Use brief and effective language.
    (b) Do not boast about yourself.

6.5 Types of Job Application Letters

- Job Application letters may be written in response to an advertisement or when you have been advised to apply by a professor, a counselor or a well wisher. Such an application is called a **solicited application letter**. In case of a solicited application letter, while answering advertisements, some reference to the advertisement must be made, usually in the subject heading or in the opening paragraph. If the application uses an introduction by a person this should also appear in the first paragraph.

- You could also be interested in a particular type of job and so may write a **prospecting or unsolicited application letter** to a firm that has not yet announced any job openings. Remember the jobs and positions can be created for talented individuals. In an unsolicited application letter you should catch the reader's interest in the first paragraph but one shouldn't ask for a job right away. Instead highlight your skills and experience and identify a specific need or area that you could contribute to.

Example of each of the above types is given below:
(1) A Solicited Application Letter

> IVY - B, Park City,
> Bilimora,
> Navsari-396 321.
> 5th February, 2014.
>
> Mr. Mukesh Lagdhir
> Sr. Accounts Manager
> CSV IND LTD.
> Vasai (E)
> Mumbai – 400 002.
>
> Dear Sir,
> **Post of Junior Accountant**
>
> I am applying for the position of an Accountant advertised in the Times of India, dated 10th January, 2014. I will be appearing for the final year B. Com examination in March and plan to appear for the C.A. intermediate examination thereafter.
>
> The B.Com curriculum has given me the necessary theoretical background in Accountancy and Financial Management. Moreover as a CA student and article clerk I have also acquired practical experience in auditing and income tax computation. I can interpret and analyse data to prepare accurate financial statements. I am familiar with accounting packages like Tally and MS office and can create computer graphics to provide reliable accounting data.
>
> I have been an article clerk for two years with M/s Kakaria Associates Co., Chartered Accountants, Vapi and have been commended for my hard work and efficiency. In college I was in the organising committee of the inter-collegiate cultural festival and successfully handled the responsibility of treasurer.
>
> The enclosed resume summarises my qualifications. I look forward to meeting you and discuss in details on any working day after 4 p.m.
>
> Yours faithfully,
> Ranu Mishra
> Encl.: Resume

(2) An Unsolicited Application Letter

Flat No. 101, Maples-A,
Park City,
Silvassa (E)
D. & N. H. 396 320

3rd March, 2014
Mr. Divyaraj Rathod
General Manager (Marketing)
Off-Link Road,
Bandra,
Mumbai – 400 005

Dear Sir,

For the past five years I have been an executive in the Marketing Department of Bauch & Laumb Ltd., Silvassa. I am now looking for a change to improve my prospects. I feel that a well-known organisation like as yours might be able to use my services.

I am 27 years old. and I graduated with first class from the S.S.R College of Arts, Commerce and Science, Silvassa. At the postgraduate level, my specialisation is Marketing and was awarded a first class degree by the University of Pune. I have also successfully completed a diploma course in Marketing from the SSR Institute of Management & Research, Silvassa.

As a part of my summer internship I had thoroughly enjoyed working with the Vision Marketing Pvt. Ltd., a reputed market research firm. My work involved researching consumer trends. I am familiar with the methods employed in demand forecasting and understanding the market trends. I would be happy if given an opportunity to work with your esteemed organisation and further continue this type of research. I am looking forward for an interview where I can give you further detailed information.

Yours faithfully,
Niku Saha.
Encl.: Resume

6.6 Bio-Data/ Resume/ Curriculum Vitae

Bio-data is a biographical data and a factual statement about life and work experiences. Bio-data gives a valid and reliable means to predict future performance based on an applicant's past performance.

A **resume** is a short, concise document that states relevant information regarding your education, skills, experiences, accomplishments and job-related interests. A resume highlights your accomplishments to show a potential employer that you are qualified for the position you are seeking. It is NOT a biography of everything you have done. The average time spent reviewing a resume is 12-15 seconds. There are several basic types of resumes used to apply for job openings. Depending on your personal circumstances, choose a chronological, functional, combination, or a targeted resume.

A **curriculum vitae** (CV) provides a summary of one's experience and skills. They are typically longer than resumes (at least two or three pages), and are used almost exclusively in countries outside of the United States. CVs include information on one's academic background, including teaching experiences, degrees, research, awards, publications, presentations and other achievements.

In a resume, the principle of **AIDA** comes in to play:

The first task – Catch the Attention: This is achieved through use of key words, proper structure and layout and visual appeal.

The second task- Create an Interest: This is achieved if the resumes showcase your uniqueness as a candidate and your benefits as a product.

The third task – Stir the Desire: This is achieved by correctly identifying the exact need and your resume must convey how you can address that need. The recruiter while going through your resume must feel a "need" for you.

The fourth, final and key task – Elicit an Action: The action that you are pursuing is, of course, to get the call for the interview.

Resume Format

Your resume creates the first impression on the prospective employer, therefore it is important to choose a format that reflects your style. Of course, do not get carried away in the effort of making a personal statement.

There are basically three formats that you may choose from:
1. The chronological format
2. The functional format
3. The hybrid format

The Chronological Format

The chronological format is the traditional format in resume writing. It enlists events in a chronological order, i.e. most recent job is given first and then moves backwards. This format is appropriate and is long and closely related to your job objective. The use of chronological format is recommended when -

    (a) you are applying for a position in the same field
    (b) your career graph shows a clear growth and a steady progress and
    (c) you have no gaps in your employment.

A chronological format creates a concise picture of the candidate and makes it easy for the employer to assess the suitability of the candidate.

The Functional Format

A functional format resume highlights your functions, skills, achievements and responsibilities which will help you do the job better. A functional format is an arrangement in which the work experience is organised in the resume by type of functions like, accounting or supervising performed or type of skills like communication or interpersonal skills. This format is appropriate when you are changing or moving in to an entirely different line of work or taking up employment after a long gap. Functional formats highlights the relevant strengths and skills of the candidate for the employer. However, on the flip side, it does not provide a detailed work history and may be disadvantageous in certain cases.

The Hybrid Format

The hybrid resume format is a combination of the chronological format and the functional format. It combines your experience and skills set. Hybrid format is used when

(a) when you have varied and unrelated work experience

(b) you have short work history

(c) you want to highlight relevant internships and other assignments.

6.7 Examples of Bio-Data, Resume and CV

Example 1: Bio-Data

Name of the Candidate	Mr. Divyaraj Rathod
Education	Bachelor of Engineering from Govt. College of Engineering, (Pune, MS), India in June 2009 securing 73%. Passed H.S.C. from Maharashtra Board Securing 76% in June 2005 Passed S.S.C. from Maharashtra Board Securing 86% in June 2003
Operating Systems/Languages/Software & Tools	Windows XP/Vista, Visual Basic 6.0/5.0, MS-SQL Server (7.0), Oracle 9.0, MS-Office 2007. ASP, C,C++ , .NET, Java Script
Experience Summary	Over two years of experience in the Information Technology Field.
Languages	English, Hindi, Marathi, Gujarati
Date of Birth	24th December 1988
Address	201, Shrusti Apartment, Plot 10, Naroli, D. & N.H. – 396230
Contact Number	0260 - 222666, 9898779898
E-mail ID	devurathod@rediffmail.com

Example 2: Resume

Resume

Kareena Kapoor
Age: 22 years
Ph No.: +919898779977
Address: Ganeshkhind,
Pune,
Maharashtra   **(MBA - Finance)**

CAREER OBJECTIVE

To become successful in life by securing employment with one of the outstanding organisations that can utilise my skills and abilities gained by my educational qualifications and practical experience.

ACADEMIC BACKGROUND

Degree/Course	Institute	Board/ University	Year	Grade
MBA	SSR Institute of Management & Research	Pune university	2013	75%
BBA	SSR College of Arts, Commerce & Science	Pune university	2012	73%
12th (HSC)	Kendriya Vidhyalaya	CBSE	2009	64%
10th (SSC)	Kendriya Vidhyala	CBSE	2007	64%

ACADEMIC PROJECTS

Projects	Organisation	Tenure	Title and brief description
1	Global Wind Power ltd	2 months	A study of Financial performance analysis with reference to global wind power ltd.

COMPUTER / TECHNICAL KNOWLEDGE

Tally 9.0
MS Office
SAP

EXTRA CURRICULAR ACTIVITIES

Participated in Inter-college singing completion
Actively worked as member of NSS Unit

AWARDS AND ACHIEVEMENTS

Best student award in the year 2012
Management Guru Award in the year 2013

SKILLS SETS

- Excellent Communication Skills
- Strong Problem solving ability
- Good grip over finance Management

PERSONAL VITAE

Date of Birth   : 25th December, 1992
Language Known :   English, Hindi, Marathi, Gujarati
Hobbies   :   Reading, singing, listening to music

Example 3: Curriculum Vitae.

Curriculum Vitae

SANTOSH KUMAR,
Mobile No: 21-99999999
E-mail: ssss@ssssl.com
CAREER OBJECTIVE:

Seeking a position to utilise my skills and abilities in the Information Technology Industry, that offers Professional growth while being resourceful, innovative and flexible.

PERSONAL SUMMARY

A successful chartered accountant with valuable experience in financial reporting and accounting covering a variety of industries from start-up business, to financial management and company closures. Also having rich experience in providing professional advice in strategic sectors such as financial reporting, taxation, auditing, corporate finance and insolvency.

CAREER HISTORY
  Chartered Accountant – Kakaria Associates

March 2008 till date
- In- charge of the company at a time of rapid expansion
- Responsible for monitoring profitability.
- Involved in the daily overseeing and management of the company's financial systems and budgets.
- Organising and maintaining accurate company accounting records.
- Analysing financial data and preparing financial statements and accounting information and reports for senior managers and directors and proposing recommendations.

- Investigating and dealing with financial irregularities.
- Necessary liaising with banks and other financial institutions.
- Supervising junior members of staff and trainee accountants.
- Instrumental in helping to turn around a loss making department.
- Involved in re-negotiating major agreements.
- Communicating with external outsourcing partners to implement improvements to accounting practices.
- Holding monthly meetings to review overhead reports with departmental heads.

Financial Planner – Paper Products Limited
June 2006 - March 2008

In charge of the analysis of revenue, margins and operating expenses for the company as well as forecasting and budgetary issues.
- In-charge of feasibility studies on potential company investments.
- Involved in the preparation of budgets and monitoring the company's profit and loss.
- Regular monitoring of the company's investments and finances and reporting these to senior managers.
- Overseeing the preparation of tax returns and the books of accounts.
- Responsible for managing the firm's payroll, stock control and credit control.
- Controlling the expenditure of the company.
- Providing advice on tax planning and VAT.
- Cash books and bank reconciliations.
- Processing and chase receipts for sales invoices.
- Responsible for journal preparation for bank, payroll, accruals, salary etc.
- In charge of Client and Supplier payments.
- Producing expense reports and investigating variances.

PROFESSIONAL EXPERIENCE
Accounting
- An excellent understanding of the technical aspects of accounting.
- Experience of liaising with internal and external auditors.
- Extensive knowledge of Enterprise-wide Resource Planning (ERP).
- Successful at resolving accounting disparities in a firm.
- Aware of all new legislation, compliance with existing regulatory requirements.
- Good working knowledge of SAP
- Possessing strong technical skills in both management and financial accounting and comfortable utilising financial information systems.
- Debt analysis and review.
- The ability to maintain clear and accurate records.

Management
- Being in charge of a company's entire financial operations.
- Management of financial systems.
- Chairing meetings with existing and potential clients.
- Experience of being involved in the recruitment and interview process of new staff.
- Proven ability to devise ways to increase a company's profitability and growth.
- Able to work individually with minimal supervision or as part of a team.
- Ability to work to tight deadlines and control a number of projects at a time.
- The ability to communicate financial issues to non financial senior management and directors.

ACADEMIC QUALIFICATIONS
CIMA Institute of Chartered Accountants of India - 2005

REFERENCES - Available on request.
PERSONAL DETAILS

Date of Birth: 19 /11/ 1980
Marital Status: Married
Address: 5588, Santosh Bhavan, College Road, Nasik-560100.

Points to Remember

- An application letter aims at highlighting the applicant's potential and secure an interview, where the candidate can elaborate on his or her usefulness to the organisation. An Application letter has to stand out among hundreds of applications received by recruiters.

- **Contents of Job Application letter**
    1. Name and address of the applicant
    2. Name and address of employer
    3. Salutation
    4. Introductory paragraph
    5. Body of the Letter of Application
    6. Concluding Paragraph

- **Types of Job application letters**
    1. Solicited application letters
    2. Unsolicited or prospecting application letters

- Bio-data is a factual statement about life and work experiences. Bio-data gives a valid and reliable means to predict future performance based on an applicant's past performance.
- A **resume** is a short, concise document that states relevant information regarding your education, skills, experiences, accomplishments, and job-related interests.
- A **curriculum vitae** (CV) provides a summary of one's experience and skills.
- In a resume the principle of **AIDA** comes in to play -
  A - Attention
  I - Interest
  D - Desire
  A - Action
- **Three resume formats:**
  1. The chronological format
  2. The functional format
  3. The hybrid format

FREQUENTLY ASKED QUESTIONS FROM UNIVERSITY OF PUNE EXAMINATIONS

1. Draft an application for the post of sales manager in Sudarshan Chemical Ltd. Pune. **[April 2006]**
2. Write a Job Application Letter to TELCO in response to an advertisement for the post of an Accountant. **[April 2008]**
3. State the contents of a Job Application **[April 2010]**
4. Write short notes
   (a) Elements of Application Letters **[April 2012]**
5. What do you mean by Job Application Letter? Describe in detail the contents of a Job Application Letters. **[April 2013]**
6. Write an Application Letter in response to the following advertisement.

WANTED

Post: Chief Account Officer
Qualification: Chartered Accountant
Package: ₹ 12, 00,000 p.a.
Send your application letter to the Recruitment Officer of Sandvik Limited, Pune-Mumbai Road, and Pune.

***

Chapter ... 7

INTERNAL AND OTHER CORRESPONDENCE

Contents ...

7.1 Office Memos (Memorandums)
- 7.1.1 Meaning of Memos
- 7.1.2 Classification of Memorandum
- 7.1.3 Parts of Memorandum
- 7.1.4 Drafting of Memorandum
- 7.1.5 Advantages and Disadvantages of Memorandum
- 7.1.6 Examples of Memorandum

7.2 Office Orders
- 7.2.1 Meaning and Drafting of Office Orders
- 7.2.2 Examples of Office Orders

7.3 Office Circulars
- 7.3.1 Meaning of Office Circulars
- 7.3.2 Features of Office Circulars
- 7.3.3 Drafting of Office Circulars
- 7.3.4 Examples of Office Circulars

7.4 Form Memos or Form Letters
- 7.4.1 Meaning
- 7.4.2 Advantages of Form Messages
- 7.4.3 Kinds of Forms
- 7.4.4 Examples

7.5 Press Release
- 7.5.1 Meaning of Press Release
- 7.5.2 Examples of Press Release

- Points to Remember

Learning Objectives ...

- To learn about Office Memorandums – classification, parts, drafting, advantages and examples
- To learn about Office Orders and learning how to draft an office order
- To study about Office circulars and understanding their features, advantages, examples etc
- To learn about the form memos or form letters
- To understand all about Press release

Introduction

Communication is a vital aspect of the managerial process. In fact, success of any business depends upon a vivid communication system used by a business house or a firm or a company in order to keep in touch with its customers. Similarly, superior - sub-ordinate relation in an office cannot thrive without having effective and meaningful communication.

Internal communication takes place within the organisation and could be -
- individual to individual,
- individual to group,
- group to individual,
- department to department

It could be oral or written, visual or audio-visual, formal or informal, and upward or downward.

Internal communication serves to inform, instruct, educate, develop, motivate, entertain, and control people in the organisation. Knowledge, goal orientation, sharing of corporate concerns, review and monitoring, performance appraisal, counseling, and training are the issues that internal communication addresses.

There are four major types of internal communication-
- Memorandum
- Office orders
- Circulars
- Office notes

7.1 Office Memos (Memorandums)

7.1.1 Meaning of Memos

Memorandum (plural memoranda or memorandums) is also known as Memo. Often called inter – office memorandum, it is a short piece of writing generally used by the officers of an organisation for communicating among them. An inter-office memo is a written communication between employees and /or employer within the same company.

A memorandum is by definition, *"a written statement that you prepare specially for a person or committee in order to give them information about a particular matter"*. It has been derived from the Latin word 'memorare', changed to 'memorandus' (notable), and means literally to 'mention' or 'tell'.

A memo can be used-

1. To issue instructions to the staff.
2. To communicate policy changes to the staff.
3. To give/ seek suggestions.
4. To request help or information.
5. To confirm a decision arrived at on the telephone.
6. To intimate granting/withholding permission to do something.
7. To seek explanation on some matter of conduct, etc.

However, a memo may not be found appropriate if the matter is of a complex or serious nature involving lengthy discussion. A memo can be filed for future reference.

7.1.2 Classification of Memorandum

The classification of memorandum is shown in figure below:

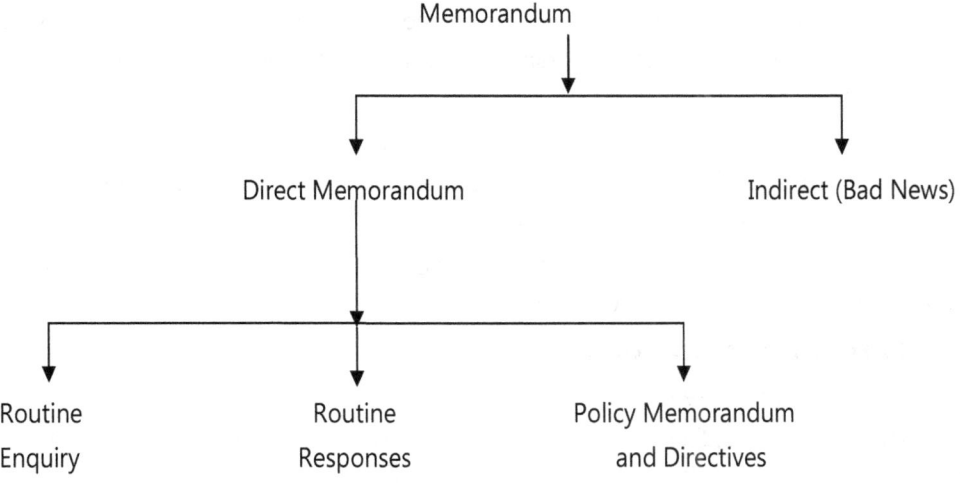

Fig. 7.1: Types of Memorandums

1. Direct Memorandum

(i) Routine Enquiries: It proceeds directly to the overall request and then systematically covers all the vital points. It stresses on logical arrangements and clear expressions. The memorandum begins directly with the objective. The necessary explanation follows. Then the specific information needed is listed in logical order. It ends with courteous words.

(ii) Routine Responses: In this case, the information is for work needs and involves no personal feelings on the part of either communicant. For this reason, the memorandum appropriately follows the direct order. It presents its contents in an orderly way, arranging them by the general topics involved (transportation, room and board, etc.), where the writing is simple and clear.

(iii) Policy Memorandums and Directives: Company policies and directives such as internal written messages giving work rules, procedures, instructions, may be written in memorandum form. These are formal documents; therefore, they should be direct, clearly written, and well organised. To make them stand out, the rules and procedures often are numbered or arranged in outline form.

Often they are compiled into policy manuals – perhaps kept in loose-leaf form in a notebook and updated as new memorandums are issued.

The memorandum begins directly with words that tell the nature of the message. The points covered are numbered for emphasis and easy understanding by employees at all levels. The memorandum ends with the president's personal appeal for compliance.

2. Indirect (Bad-News) Memorandums

Memorandums that convey negative news are not rare in business. It requires indirect and diplomatic treatment. Most memorandums communicate information that is of little personal concern to the people involved.

Personal Messages require tactful handling. This means treating them – with explanation, justification or such, paving the way for the bad news. It means watching words carefully, trying to emphasise the positive over the negative.

Memos that convey bad news need to be written inductively, with a positive tone. But bear in mind that being inductive is not synonymous with being ambiguous.

7.1.3 Parts of Memorandum

Memo has following three parts:

1. Heading: The heading consists of information about the organisation, the type of document being written, who wrote it, when it was written, who the intended audience is, and the subject of the document. Make sure you address the reader by his or her correct name and job title. Be specific and concise in your subject line. The heading segment follows this general format:

To: Name and position of the reader.

From: Name and position of the writer.

Subject: A phrase that focuses the reader's attention on the subject of the memo.

Date: Date the memo is sent.

2. **Body:** The body of the memo has two parts:
   - the purpose statement
   - the explanation.

As the reader of the memo is often very busy, he/she is not likely to read the memo closely. Therefore, the first sentence should state the whole message of the memo. This sentence is like an abstract to a report. One should not begin a memo with background information and work gradually to the main point. Instead the main point should come first and then the background and explanation of the message in fuller detail should follow. If the purpose of the memo is to ask someone to do something, that request should be in the first sentence. If the memo's purpose is to announce something, the gist of the announcement should be in the first sentence.

3. **Conclusion:** The conclusion summarises the memo and ties up any loose ends. The summary restates the topic of the memo in 1-2 sentences. The polite closure offers the best way to contact the writer to ask questions, to look at samples, or to talk story. One is often tempted to end the memo with a "cordially yours" and a signature, but these are not necessary and are usually excluded. Because memos are usually short, it is seldom necessary even to write a conclusion or summary; however, if the memo happens to be more than a page long, a summary may be in order.

7.1.4 Drafting of Memorandum

Various guidelines for drafting memo are as follows:

1. **Legality of Document:** Memos are legal documents. That is why it is important to write them in a professional manner. The legality of the document also enhances the importance of professionalism within a memo.

2. **List Recipients of the Memo:** It is considerate to inform the readers of who all is receiving the memo you have written. This way the readers know who the informed audience is and who has this information.

3. **Use an Informative Subject Line:** Be specific from the beginning; tell the reader what the subject of the memo is and what aspect of the subject is going to be discussed. Let the reader know if the memo is a proposal, progress report, question, or result.

4. **Use Strong Opening Sentences:** Like a subject line the first few sentences need to elaborate on the topic and purpose of the memo.

5. **Make the End the Beginning:** Putting the most important information at the beginning of the document ensures that the reader understands the purpose of the document. Put what you want the reader to get out of the memo at the top and then continue to go into more detail in the body of the memo. This is known as an inverted pyramid style of writing.

6. **Keep it Personal:** Memos always have a conversational style, and use words like "I", "you", and "we". It sounds more natural to say, "I would like you to do this" And it is more personal because you are addressing a specific individual.
7. **Keep it simple:** Avoid words that might not be known to readers.
8. **Become the Reader:** Keep your reader in mind when you are writing a memo. One tip for achieving a reader-centered memo is to pretend that you are having a face to face conversation with the memo recipient.
9. **Call to Action:** Close your memo with a call to action. It's simple: if you want a response by Friday at 3 p.m., then say so. This gives the reader an obligation to send you something back.
10. **Closing:** The closing in a memo is as simple as a signature line. The signature line needs to include a contact phone number, e-mail address, and, if your company has a web URL, that should be included too. A closing line, if needed or not, will depend on your relationship with the recipient.
11. **Dates:** Make sure you write any dates in the following format – month in written format (e.g., December), followed by the day in numerical format, concluding with the year in numerical format. This format is important so that dates are not confused. If the memo is sent to another country, the date will not be misinterpreted.
12. **Check before you send:** Take time before you send the memo to make sure that you have covered all the correct information. Double check names, dates, and the particulars of the project/topic to make sure that everything is accurate and up to date.

7.1.5 Advantages and Disadvantages of Memorandum

Advantages of memo are given as follows:-

1. **Brief:** It is the basic communication. It includes nothing except the message in its simplest form.
2. **Convenient:** The chief notations at the top give details about the addressee, the writer, the subject and the date. The memo number is also there. Major area on the page is left free for the message, which can be typed, or hand written.
3. **Inexpensive:** Since it is for use within the organisation, no expensive stationery need to be used for it. If computer facilities are available, computer memos on the monitor would be still cheaper.
4. **Future Reference:** Depending upon its importance, a memo can be destroyed after being read, or filed or stored on computer disc for future reference.

Disadvantages of Memorandum

Disadvantages of memo are given as follows:

1. Responses cannot be received instantly.
2. Sometimes suggestions are given through memo, and then people usually neglect the information.

7.1.6 Example of Memorandum

Example 1: Memo to the Sectional Heads, announcing appointment of a person from outside to the post of Personnel Manager.

19th November, 2012

To: Sectional Heads

From: Anuj Kumar

Managing Director

Rayon Pharma Ltd.

Subject: Appointment of Personnel Manager

I am pleased to share with you that we have recruited a new personnel manager for our company. Mr. Rajesh Solanki has accepted the position effective from November 25, 2012. Rajesh comes to us with a wealth of experience. He was previously the personnel Manager at Lake Shore Medical Hospital, where he supervised the performance of the human resources. He also handled the recruitment and selection there, reviewed and analysed the promotion policies, and helped conceptualise training and development concepts. The Board has decided to hire him, keeping in view that we have some deserving internal candidates for this post, but they are outperforming in their present post and the board does not want any change in that structure. We are excited about his decision to join the organisation. Please join us in welcoming him to the Company in his new role.

Anuj Kumar

Managing Director

Rayon Pharma Ltd.

Gandhinagar

Example 2: A memo inviting views and suggestions.

Memorandum	For Action	Please
	comment	display
From: The Managing Director	information	file
To: Personnel Managers	discussion	return
		pass to
Date: 15 April, 2006		……

Subject: Installation of clocking – in machines

The Board is thinking of installing an automatic clocking-in system in the offices of each division. Before we do this we need to know:

1. How the arrangements concerning the breaks, especially lunch breaks, have been working.
2. How many machines we would need.
3. Whether time now lost through bad time-keeping would be saved. Can you provide us with your views on:
   - How the staff will react to the idea.
   - How we can deal with the union on the matter.

If possible, I would like to receive your report before the next Board Meeting i.e. on 1 June.

Example 3: A memo to an employee informing him of a cut in his salary.

VIJAYA BANK LTD.
Udaipur
Date: 19th April, 2013
Ref.: 7.40-STF – 1786:2013
To: Mr. R. Krishna, Clerk
From: P. K. Sharma, Manager

You remained away from your duties on the date/s and for the period/s mentioned below. Please note that you have not earned salary and emoluments for the said period.

DATE:	Period
April 18, 2013	10:30 a.m. to 5:30 p.m.

This is without prejudice to our right to take disciplinary action against you.

P. K. Sharma
C.C. To,
1. Staff Section, East Zone,
2. Salary Section.

Example 4: A memo to an employee asking for explanation for going on leave without prior permission.

VIJAYA BANK LTD.
Udaipur

Date: April 7, 2013
Ref.: VIG: 1431: A-13
To: Mr. Manish Desai, Clerk
From: D. K. Sharma, Manager

Sub.: Your absence from 15-3-2013 to 20-3-2013
Ref. Your telegram and letters dated 15-3-2013 and 22-3-2013

(1) We note that you sent a telegram from Jaipur on 16th March requesting medical leave from 15-3-2013 to 20-3-2013 and later submitted an application for leave from 15-3-2013 to 20-3-2013 producing a medical certificate from a doctor practicing at Jaipur. Please let us know whether you had obtained prior permission to leave station.
(2) In your application you have stated that you were suffering from viral fever. But your medical certificate says you had leg sprain. Will you please explain the discrepancy?

If your reply does not reach us on or before April 10, 2013 your absence will be treated as one without leave and will incur loss of pay.

D. K. Sharma

KVS/BN
cc. To the Branch Manager, Udaipur

Example 5: Memo regarding a disciplinary matter.

Memorandum
No. CS/60/7
Dated: 21/6/2013

It has come to notice that Shri. C. S. Mehra, Sales Officer, working with the Navsari Branch of the company has been found to be indulging in the following unwarranted activities:
(a) Passing out secret information regarding the manufacture of the company's production to competitors.
(b) Giving out wrong information such as quoting the old rates of the company's product in place of revised rates, expressing uncertainty about the supply of company's product to the customers and so on;

(c) Indulging in loose talk with colleagues and outsiders about the company's management;
(d) Talking about imaginary deficiencies in the company's product and giving good opinion of competitors before the company's customers with a view to giving bad name to the company's product.

Shri C. S. Mehra is hereby directed to explain his conduct in the above regard, and his explanation in writing should reach the undersigned on or before 25/6/2003. Failure to furnish his explanation within the time given shall be treated as his inability to state anything further and that he has accepted his conduct as spelt out above.

Sd/-
General Manager (Sales)
Shri C. S. Mehra, Navsari Branch
Through : Branch Manager, Navsari

7.2 Office Orders

7.2.1 Meaning and Drafting of Office Orders

Office orders, as the term suggests, are communications of a different type. Office order is a tool of down ward communication; it travels from the higher-ups down to the subordinates. The word order suggests acceptance or compliance. If a message is conveyed as an order, it means that it carries a stamp of authority with it and has to be accepted.

They are meant to communicate matters relating to
- certain rights,
- withdrawing rights,
- imposing restrictions,
- making postings/ transfers, promotions,
- retrenchment,
- granting annual increment,
- withholding increment,
- disciplinary action, etc.

Orders in writing can only be issued by superiors. They are, therefore, clear examples of downward communication. The drafting of the order is done by subordinates but it is submitted to the concerned higher officer for his perusal and approval with or without the necessary changes. Great care is needed in the drafting of office orders. They are supposed to be very precise and inoffensive. It has to be ensured that neither the recipient of the order nor any other person to whom the copy of the order is sent raises any objection. Especially sensitive issues must be tackled very carefully, keeping in mind all the consequences that they may lead to. That is why it is advisable to use clear and concise, familiar and unambiguous expressions. Idioms and phrases had better be avoided. Order should clearly specify who they are meant for. Some orders are sent to the concerned individuals with copies to the concerned department; others may be meant for display on the notice boards.

7.2.2 Examples of Office Orders

Examples 1: A Transfer Order

DHARMACHAKRA MOTORS LTD.
VANSDA - 11001
Date: 12 April, 2013
Ref.: 64/03/per

ORDER

Mr. Sajan Shah has been transferred to the Personnel Department. He shall report to the personnel Manager latest by 18 April, 2013 after handing over charges of his duties to the Superintendent (Administration).

Sd/-
Chetan S
(Admin Officer)
CC:
Accounts officer
Superintendent (Admin.)

Example 2: Suspension order.

JAIN TUBE CO.
VAPI
Date: 25 April, 2013
Ref.: 16/13

ORDER

Shri Raj Adhikari, Accounts Clerk is suspended from the services of the company with immediate effect. He shall, however, be entitled to draw subsistence allowance according to the rules of the company.

Shri Raj Adhikari shall not be allowed entry into the premises of the company except for the limited purpose of attending the disciplinary proceedings before the enquiry officer.

Sd/-
Rakesh Chalke
Personnel Manager
CC:
Notice Board
All Departments.

Example 3: Order Granting special increments.

Min Toys Pvt. Ltd.
Silvassa
Date: 28-4-13
Ref.: PRI/15/13

ORDER

In recognition of the meritorious performance of Shri Nikunj Jain, the management is pleased to grant him a special increment of ₹ 3000 w.e.f. 1.5.2013.

Sd/-
Jaykumar
Manager (Personnel)
CC:
Accounts officer

Example 4: Order reinstating a suspended employee.

JAIN TUBE CO.
VAPI
Date: 29 April, 2013

Ref.: Per/18/13

ORDER

Pursuant to the finding contained in the report of the Enquiry Officer Shri Keyur Bhalani, Shri Raj Adhikari, Accounts Clerk is reinstated in the services of the company. The order number Per/16/13 of 25 April, 2013 suspending him from services stands revoked with immediate effect.

Sd/-
Personnel Manager

CC:
Notice Board/ All Departments

7.3 Office Circulars

7.3.1 Meaning of Office Circulars

A circular is in the form of a letter addressed to all offices branches or departments of a company and is drafted in such a way that the information is useful and understandable to all concerned. The purpose of the circular is to circulate the information contained therein. Whenever the management has to inform anything to the entire organisation, or may be to a department, it uses office circulars. Further, a circular may be issued for various purposes ranging from invitation to the office staff for a party to information about the installation of a card punching machine in the office.

7.3.2 Features of Office Circulars

- It is written in simple language free from technical jargon, as it is intended for employees across the organisation.
- It is a letter addressed by the head office to all branches and departments.
- It is a medium to carry information over a large number of people.
- Since management issues a number of circulars on many occasions, each circular has to carry a reference number which is self explanatory.

7.3.3 Drafting of Office Circulars

- A circular should be on company's letter head.
- Mention the circular number and the date.
- State the subject prominently.
- Ensure that the circular contains complete and correct information.
- Use very simple and unambiguous language.
- The circular should be signed. The designation of the issuing authority should be clearly mentioned.
- Enclose the list on which the employee's signatures are to be taken.

7.3.4 Examples of Office Circulars

Example: 1 Circular regarding a computer training programme.

ABC LTD.
SILVASSA
Date: 1st Jan. 2014
CIRCULAR NO. 345/2014

A five-hour company training programme has been arranged for all employees on Sunday 5th January, 2014 in the office premises. The programme will start at 10. a.m. All employees are required to attend the programme.

Sd/-
Manager
Human Resources

Example 2: Circular regarding cleanliness at work place.

KUNJAL PHARMA LTD.
VALSAD
Date 10 April, 2014

Circular No. 7/86

The management desires all members of staff to observe utmost cleanliness on and around the premises of the company. It has been observed that cigarette butts, disposable glasses, cups and bottles, paper napkins, and leftovers of lunch etc., are not properly disposed of by some employees. They are requested to ensure proper disposal of all waste matter and maintain cleanliness of the environment.

Sd/-
Manager

Example 3: Circular inviting suggestions.

VANSH ELECTRICALS LTD.
MULUND - 110006
Dated: 25 May, 2013

Circular No. 1435/13

The office manual which was last revised in July 1988 is now due for revision. We look forward to all employees to consider this matter with interest and send their suggestions of the undersigned latest by 25 June, 2013.

Sd/-
Manager

7.4 Form Memos or Form Letters

7.4.1 Meaning

Form memos or form letters are used when an identical message is to be sent to a large number of people. Form letters are used for external communication, form memos for internal communications.

We can use form letters to -

- Answer often-recurring enquiries.
- Acknowledge orders, payments
- Make simple adjustments,
- Invite candidates for a test / interview,
- Make appointments
- Promote goodwill
- Give news to customers, stockholders, suppliers, etc.

Form memos may be used to -

- Give news to employees,
- Deal with disciplinary matters,
- Deal with leave and other service conditions of employees,
- Simplify office procedures, etc.

7.4.2 Advantages of Form Messages

Form messages enjoy certain obvious advantages-

1. **They save time:** A master draft is prepared and is duplicated at an automatic machine. Within seconds we get as many copies as needed.
2. **They save money:** Sending a typewritten message to every individual would prove quite expensive. If we calculate the cost of man hours saved by sending form messages, we shall discover that form messages are very economical.
3. **They can be of better quality:** If letters are written by dissatisfied, incompetent or overworked subordinates, they are poor and shabby both in content and appearance. But if competent people are entrusted with the responsibility of preparing and typing the master draft, the form message may turn out to be very impressive.
4. **They facilitate mailing campaigns:** It would be impossible to think of a large –scale mailing campaign (where thousands of customers have to be contacted simultaneously), if a personal, separately typed letter were to be sent to each individual.

7.4.3 Kinds of Forms

Four kinds of forms are in use.

1. **Complete form:** In a complete form, the messages are identical in every word. If it is a form letter, the general salutation is Dear student, Dear Customer, Dear Subscriber, etc. In a form memo, the word To is followed by such terms as All staff members, All employees, the heads of all sections, etc.
2. **Fill –in forms:** In this form, messages are prepared in advance to meet specific kinds of situations with blank spaces are left for filling in variable information. If the blanks are filled in at the same electronic typewriter or computer on which the original form was prepared, the fill-ins will be hardly noticeable and the addressee will get a 'personalised' letter.
3. **Guide form:** Here, model letters or memos are prepared in advance to meet various kinds of situations. Whenever someone has to write a similar message, he/she can adopt the model to meet the specific situation.
4. **Paragraph form:** A letter containing a number of paragraphs or a booklet of paragraphs to respond to different situations is kept ready. When a reply is to be sent, relevant paragraph(s) is /are ticked and the letter mailed. Or the communicator marks relevant paragraph(s) in the booklet and dictates a couple of paragraphs to personalise the letter. The typist then types the letter giving a suitable order to the paragraphs. In this way, even lengthy messages are prepared in a short time.

7.4.4 Examples of Forms

Example 1: A form letter inviting a candidate for interview

Dear Sir/ Madam

With reference to your application for the post of .... you are required to present yourself for an interview at this office at........................... on ....

Please note that you will be appearing at the interview at your own expense and no T.A. or D.A. is admissible.

Yours faithfully,

Example 2: A form memo intimating the Branch office the confirmation of an employee.

PARTH PLACEMENTS
H.O. Bharuch
OFFICE MEMO

Date: _____
To,

From:

Dear Sir/ Madam

Mr. / Mrs. / Miss.........................
We are pleased to inform you that Mr. /Mrs./Miss......................... has been confirmed in his/her existing capacity as......................... with effect from .... Consequently, he/she would be eligible to the benefits of provident fund as per rules from the said date. He/she has been allotted provident fund account No. ....
He/she is advised to return the enclosed provident fund forms duly filled in and signed by him/her.
Pleased inform Mr. /Mrs. / Miss......................... accordingly.

Yours faithfully,

7.5 Press Release

Introduction

On numerous occasions and for important reasons, an organisation has to reach out to the world at large. Written communication aimed at the world outside the organisation is a very important way of projecting the company's image. It can be through personal correspondence, an advertisement offering the company's products and services, an advertisement for a new member of staff in press, notices in the business or professional press and journals, an article or details in the local/national press concerning the company and its activities passed on to the press by the company itself. It might also be by a mail shot, a printed letter or card sent out to thousands of potential customers, or slipped into magazines by arrangement with the publishers, detailing some special promotion or sales drive.

All these communications have the advantage of being able to reach a large number of people and hence they should be prepared with care and concern so as to convey the right tone, attitude and information in the style of language most suitable for the target audience or the market aimed at.

7.5.1 Meaning of Press Releases

When a company has some information it wishes to make public, someone with the authority to do so will prepare a press release. The secretary will no doubt be asked to present it in an easily readable format (perhaps on a form specially headed for the purpose).

Most of the newspapers have some space reserved for corporate news and public notice. The news editor whosoever, reserves the right to publish the matter sent to him intact or after editing it, in order that the press releases appear as it is intended to be. Care must be taken to observe the following points.

(a) **Substantial information:** The press release must be newsworthy. It is supposed to be an objective statement of some fact, some decision taken. The matter to be published should, therefore, be free from trappings of journalism.

(b) **Clarity:** A press release must be written out in a clear and transparent style. In choice of words, therefore, suggestions must be avoided in favour of denotation.

(c) **Brevity:** It goes without saying that a press release must be as brief as possible. Only then it will be clear. Moreover, the editor has no time to prune the matter. The newspaper has also to accommodate a large number of notices and other such items in their columns.

(d) A press release should also be free from idioms, stale joke and pomposity. Its aim is to highlight something worth reporting.

(e) In a very skillful manner it may, and should, uphold the company image, but it should not obviously look like an advertisement. It should be above all informative. At the same time it can and should positively project the company image.

(f) The release must be given a carefully chosen and suitable heading.

(g) If the matter is long it should be clearly divided into paragraphs. The paragraphs may also be given sub-heading.

7.5.2 Examples of Press Releases

Example 1: A press release issued by a reputed company dismissing the consumer's fears about the shortage of its products.

VACUUM EVAPORATED

Tata Salt
IODIZED

Available throughout the country at uniform price of ₹ 6 per kg.

We are the primary and by far the largest producer of salt in the country and one of the largest in the world.

For human consumption, we produce a premium grade Vacuum-Evaporated Iodized Salt-Tata Salt – the like of which is not produced anywhere.

We market Tata Salt in one kg. packs throughout the country at a uniform price of ₹ 6 per kg and we have the largest market share.

There is absolutely no receipt of shortage of salt and the consumers are advised not to panic and not to pay more than the price printed on the pack.

In addition, we also carry very large stocks of solar – evaporated salt which we do not market at present. In the unlikely event of the need arising we can, with some government support, move this salt in large quantities to any part of the country for sale as loose salt for human consumption.

PLEASE DO NOT GIVE IN TO THE ANTI-SOCIAL ELEMENTS

TATA CHEMICALS LIMITED
The Company that cares

Example 2: A press release about a company's net profit in the corporate news.

Procter & Gamble

Procter & Gamble (P&G) India Ltd. has reported a net profit of ₹ 14.18 crore for the first quarter of financial year 1998-99. Showing an increase of 31 per cent over net profit of ₹ 10.8 crore in the last corresponding period.

The company achieved sales of ₹ 177.8 crore during the period. A growth of 10 per cent over sales of ₹ 107.2 crore in the same period last year.

In a statement issued here, B V Patel, Chairman & Managing Director of P&G India attributed the impressive profit growth to continued strong performance of the company's health care business, innovative marketing initiatives such as Vicks 'mega-branding' and strong advertising, supported by a good monsoon and effective stops to control costs and efficiencies.

Example 3: A press release about a significant change in a company.

> In a significant move, UK tobacco giant BAT has recalled Managing Director of VST Industries Ltd. Malcolm Fry and appointed Mr. Raymond S. Noronha as the now Managing Director of the company with effect from Nov. 1, 2013. Mr. Fry returns to BAT World head quarter at London UK, where he will be seconded to the Department of Trade and Industry of the British Government states the company release. Mr. S Thrumalai has also been appointed as Deputy Managing Director of the company.
>
> Hyderabad Industries Ltd. has posted a 14 per cent growth in its gross turnover to ₹ 350.8 crore for the first half of the current fiscal ended Sept. 2013. The company has achieved the gross profit of ₹ 17.47 crore during the first half as against a loss of ₹ 1.36 crore in the corresponding period of last year.
>
> With respect of VST Natural Products Ltd., the wholly owned subsidiary, the company was looking for a prospective joint venture partner and efforts were on in identify a strong partner the release added.

Points to Remember

- There are four major types of internal communication-
    - Memorandum
    - Office orders
    - Circulars
    - Office notes
- **A memorandum** is by definition, *"a written statement that you prepare specially for a person or committee in order in order to give them information about a particular matter"*.

    A memo can be used -
    1. To issue instructions to the staff
    2. To communicate policy changes to the staff
    3. To give/ seek suggestions
    4. To request help or information
    5. To confirm a decision arrived at on the telephone
    6. To intimate granting/withholding permission to do something
    7. To seek explanation on some matter of conduct, etc.
- Memorandum is classified as-
    1. Direct Memorandum - (i) routine enquiries (ii) routine responses (iii) Policy memorandums.
    2. Indirect Memorandum.

- **Parts of a memorandum-**
  - Heading
  - Body
  - Conclusion
- Drafting of Memorandum
  - Legality of document
  - List recipients of the memo
  - Use an informative subject line
  - Use strong opening sentences
  - Make the end the beginning
  - Keep it simple
  - Become the reader
  - Call to action
  - closing
  - Dates

    Check before you send
- **Advantages of Memos**
  - Brief
  - Convenient
  - Inexpensive
  - Future reference
- **Office Order** is a tool of downward communication; it travels from the higher-ups down to the subordinates. The word order suggests acceptance or compliance. If a message is conveyed as an order, it means that it carries a stamp of authority with it and has to be accepted.
- **An Office Circular** is in the form of a letter addressed to all offices branches or departments of a company and is drafted in such a way that the information is useful and understandable to all concerned.
- **Drafting of Office Circulars**
  - A circular should be on company's letter head.
  - Mention the circular number and the date.
  - State the subject prominently.
  - Ensure that the circular contains complete and correct information.

- Use very simple and unambiguous language.
- The circular should be signed. The designation of the issuing authority should be clearly mentioned.
- Enclose the list on which the employee's signatures are to be taken.

- **Form memos or form letters** are used when an identical message is to be sent to a large number of people. Form letters are used for external communication, form memos for internal communications.

- **Advantages of form messages**
    1. They save time.
    2. They save money.
    3. They can be of better quality.
    4. They facilitate mailing campaigns.

- **Kinds of Forms**
    1. Complete form.
    2. Fill-in forms.
    3. Guide form.
    4. Paragraph form.

> **Note: As this is a new chapter, there are no Pune University Examination Questions**

Chapter ... 8

NEW TECHNOLOGIES IN BUSINESS COMMUNICATION

Contents ...

Introduction
- 8.1 Internet
    - 8.1.1 E-mail
    - 8.1.2 Websites
    - 8.1.3 Electronic Clearance System (ECS)
    - 8.1.4 Writing a blog
- 8.2 Social Media Network
    - 8.2.1 Twitter
    - 8.2.2 Face book
    - 8.2.3L LinkedIn
    - 8.2.4 YouTube
    - 8.2.5 Cellular Phone /Mobile
- 8.3 Whats App
- 8.4 Voice Mail
- 8.5 Short Messaging Services
- 8.6 Video Conferencing
- • Points to Remember
- • Frequently Asked Questions from University of Pune Examination

Learning Objectives ...

- To learn about the Internet including its features like E-mail, websites, ECS, writing blogs
- To learn more about the social media network like Twitter, Facebook, LinkedIn, You Tube, Phone/ Mobile
- To understand what is Whatsapp and voice mail
- To study about short messaging services and video conferencing

Introduction

Internet is the largest network in the world that connects hundreds of thousands of individual networks all over the world. The internet, in simple terms, is a network of the interlinked computer networking worldwide, which is accessible to the general public. These interconnected computers work by transmitting data through a special type of packet switching which is known as the IP or the internet protocol.

The internet can send email messages, send or receive files between computers, surfing the web etc. The **Web (World Wide Web)** consists of information organized into Web pages containing text and graphic images. A collection of linked Web pages that has a common theme or focus is called a **Web site. Web browsers** are programs used to explore the Internet. There are many Web browser programs available including Netscape Navigator, Internet Explorer and Opera. Internet Explorer is the Internet browser made by Microsoft and comes with Windows operating system. **Email**, sometimes written as e-mail, is simply the shortened form of "electronic mail," a system for receiving, sending, and storing electronic messages. **Social media** is the social interaction among people in which they create, share or exchange information and ideas in virtual communities and networks. Some of the popular social media networks are Twitter, Facebook, LinkedIN, etc

8.1 The Internet

The internet is "international computer network" connecting other networks, computers, and servers, and is accessible to the public via modem links. Internet is the largest network in the world that connects hundreds of thousands of individual networks all over the world. The internet in simple terms is a network of the interlinked computer networking worldwide, which is accessible to the general public. It is a network of networks' that consists of millions of private and public, academic, business, and government networks linked by copper wires, fiber optic cables, wireless connections, and other technologies.

The internet has become an indispensible tool. It can be used at a basic level for email and for research, and it can be used at a more comprehensive level as a channel for selling business products and services.

A web browser is required to gain access to the Internet. It is a software application that enables a user to display and access information typically located on a web page. Microsoft's Internet Explorer, Mozilla Firefox and Google Chrome are the three leading web browsers. Once a browser is installed, access to the Internet can be obtained through an Internet service provider (ISP). The Providers may differ in the features they provide, but all will provide basic amenities such as allow one to send and receive e-mails. As with other forms of communication, there are many plans and prices from which to choose.

Applications of the Internet

The following are some applications of the Internet.

- **Email Electronic mail** (email) is a store-and- forward method of writing, sending, receiving, and saving messages over the Internet. Email has been discussed in detail later in the chapter.

- **Remote Access:** The Internet allows computer users to connect to other computers and store information easily, wherever they may be across the world. They may do this with or without the use of security, authentication, and encryption technologies, depending on the requirements. This encourages new ways of working from home, collaboration, and information sharing in many industries.
- **File Sharing:** The Internet has made it very convenient for people or organisations, separated geographically, to share information in a lot of different forms. A computer file, which contains a video, image, data, or an application, can be emailed to customers, colleagues and friends as an attachment. It can be uploaded to a website for easy download by others. It can be put into a 'shared location' for instant use by colleagues on the same network. Internet collaboration technology enables business and project teams to share documents, scheduling tools and other information. Such collaboration occurs in a wide variety of areas including scientific research, software development, conference planning, political activism, and creative writing.
- **Social networking:** Social networking through the internet is the way most people irrespective of their age communicate these days. People can gather and share information and experiences on various topics through social networking sites on the Web, such as Face book, Twitter, LinkedIn, and WAYN as well as blogs, which are usually maintained by individuals with regular entries on descriptions, events, etc. These sites allow people to remain connected to the people they know through regular feeds and updates. As against static websites of organisations or individuals that appear on the Web, social networking sites are very interactive and promise collaborations among the users.
- **Marketing:** The Internet has also made business –to-business (B2B) and business-to-consumer (B2C) marketing very easy for companies. Some of the well-known companies today, such as Amazon.com and eBay, have grown by taking advantage of the efficient nature of low-cost advertising and commerce through the Internet, also known as e-commerce. It is the fastest way to spread information to a vast target audience simultaneously. The internet has also subsequently revolutionised shopping –for example, a person can order a book online and received it in mail within a couple of days, or download it directly in some cases. Moreover, the Internet has significantly facilitated personalised cyber marketing, which allows a company to market a product to a specific person or a specific group of people more so than any other advertising medium. For instance, if the company has access to a person's browsing history and know that he/she looks mostly for flowers and books online, they can send him/her mailers only about these products and can avoid sending irrelevant information about other products that are not demanded by the prospective consumer. Although the emergence of this technology is

considered a revolution in marketing, its ethical implication is very sensitive. Debates are ensuing on the issue of accessing someone's browsing history without their knowledge and permission.

- **Education:** The Internet has also revolutionised the concept of distance learning. Institutes offering such courses host websites that offer complete information and support to students about the courses, assignments, examinations, and schedules. Some institutes also offer online assignment submissions and examinations, thereby making distance education a very pleasant experience for the student. A large number of universities offer distance learning programmes to their off-campus students. Using internet application, online/web classes are conducted for the students who may even be professionals. The software used can make such classes as interactive and dynamic at those offered face-to-face ,for example: online tutoring companies such as Tutorvista.com, Vienova, Kidspan, Planet tutor etc.

Advantages of Internet

The following list of major perceived advantages is suggestive but not exhaustive:

1. **Access to Information:** The Internet stores a huge amount of information and users have easy access to the vast amount if information available. Having ample amount of information readily available is important for the successful functioning of an organisation, and therefore any enhancement of the ability to acquire or access information can be seen as a great benefit to society.

2. **Information Spreading:** Anyone can easily and quickly post and publicise information through the internet so that the information is available to a large audience. Individuals can voice their opinions by informing and influencing others and thereby promotes freedom of speech.

3. **Communication:** The internet facilitates one-to-one, one-to-many and many-to-many communication and enables users to communicate easily and inexpensively with a wide variety of individuals across the globe. Communication goes beyond the distribution of information – it is a two way process that allows for the expression of viewpoints, the creation of intimacy, and the coordination of actions. Since communication is so important to individuals, the internet's enhancement of the power to communicate can be considered a great benefit.

4. **Production and Commerce:** By enabling coordination and partial automation of productive processes that span time and space, the internet enables new models for production. It also allows new models for trade, business and commerce. These economic benefits translate into social and cultural benefits because they provide people with new products and services, faster and easier delivery of existing products and services at less cost.

5. **Learning and Cognitive Development:** The internet is known to have a wonderful system of learning and cognitive development in place. Interactive learning styles are supported by the internet and computers and also enhance learning by supporting new mutlimedia ways of presenting information and improves the development of good sensory motor abilities.

Disadvantages of the Internet

Disadvantages of the internet are as follows:

1. **Information Overload:** The Internet is a place where users are exposed to a vast amount of information, which are often irrelevant, unclear and inaccurate. This has an adverse effect on individuals as often when the user reads this vast amount of information, they can make poor decisions, reduce their attention span, cause anxiety, and, for organisations , it leads to less efficiency and poorer decision-making.

2. **False and Harmful Information:** The internet, often contain false and unreliable information due to the absence of good selection mechanisms. The internet contains a lot of harmful information such as extremist ideology, recipes for making bombs, extreme forms of pornography, libelous information, and so forth. Moreover, it is often impossible to evaluate the correctness of the information found on the internet, as it is often difficult to credit or evaluate the sources.

3. **Harmful Effects on Production and Commerce :** It has been argued that the easy distribution of digital information over the internet will hurt commerce and the so-called culture industry (musicians, film makers, artists, etc). It has also been claimed that the internet and digital media generally, negatively affect artistic production by rationalising art and art production techniques.

4. **Harmful Effects on Identity Formation and Psychological Development:** In cyberspace, actions can be performed with utmost secrecy, which can lead to anti-social behavior that is performed without revenge. Playing violent computer games causes one to be violent and disrespectful which often goes unnoticed. The possibility of such anti-social behaviours is held to harm psychological development. Often people face no consequences for their behavior. Also, internet pornography is easily available is claimed to promote a harmful form of disinhibition that harms personalities. More generally, internet can lead to an addiction.

5. **Cultural Fragmentation:** It has been claimed that the internet promotes cultural fragmentation by stimulating the formation of virtual communities and group organised around specialised interests, theme or cultural identities.

6. **Loss of Privacy and Private-Public Boundaries:** Often the users are faced with insecurities about the privacy conditions as there is very little privacy on the internet.

8.1.1 E-mail

Introduction

E-mail is a modern miraculous invention. It is unbelievably quick and can reach anyone anywhere within a few minutes. Mail can carry documents, videos, images, graphs, audios etc. It saves lot of time as you can send the mail to many people at a time. Almost all the companies use email for their official conversation for the facilities it provides. If you work in an office, you probably write emails every day-to colleagues, to your boss, to clients etc. Even if you're still at college, you'll need to email your lecturers once in a while and many employers now expect resumes and cover letters to be sent through email. Millions of people use email every day. Executives get so many mails every day that it becomes difficult for them to read them all. Therefore they prioritise the mails and read only those mails which are important and compulsory to read. Sending a mail to someone is not difficult but getting that person to read your mail is a real challenge with emails. If your mail does not sound important for the person you are sending, he/she may send the mail directly to the trash box without even reading it. Therefore you need to draft your mail smartly so that a busy reader does not skip to read your mail.

Definition

Email or electronic mail is the process of exchanging message electronically using computers. Email allows users to communicate with each other in less time and at nominal cost. Apart from textual data, images and audio & video files can also be sent through emails.

Advantages of E-mail

1. **Speed:** Without a doubt, speed and ease of delivery are the major advantages of e-mail. Although a fax offers these too, the print quality of a fax is often poor.
2. **Storage:** E-mail has other advantage over a fax. A fax from a fax machine cannot be stored electronically. E-mail is stored in the recipient's computer even if he is not present.
3. **Multiple Copies:** E-mail is easy because there is no hard copy to deal with. It's great for reaching a lot of readers for example, all 10,000 employees in a large company at once.
4. **Cost:** The cost of sending or receiving e-mail message is considered very low. Email can be sent internationally easily and is less expensive than a letter.
5. **Auditing:** Even the simplest e-mail package will provide a number of features that allow users to audit their messages. Most programs will allow users to keep copies of any messages they produce, automatically marking them with the date and time they were created.
6. **Multimedia:** The latest e-mail packages allow users to include multimedia elements in their message. Messages can include a variety of different elements such as graphics, video and sound files.

7. **Flexibility:** The hardware and software used for handling e-mail can also be used for a variety of other purposes. A typical modem, for example, can also be used to send or receive fax messages.
8. **Group Work:** E-mail facilities group work and remote working. Group work involves several people working on the same project. Electronic mail enables them to communicate with each other and share data files. People working way from a central office can be in touch/contact with the central office through e-mail.

Disadvantages of E-mail

1. **Loss of Format**: E-mail is fast and convenient, but when you get rid of paper, you may get rid of other things along with it, such as the format. Because of the variety of communication software packages, the format of an e-mail message often gets scrambled in transmission. Sentences are often cut short and dropped to the next line, which can be irritating.
2. **Security**: Unless they are encrypted, e-mail messages can be intercepted relatively easily. Many companies openly admit that they monitor employees' e-mail. This makes e-mail unsuitable for sending confidential information unless special precautions are taken.
3. **Cost:** In order to send or receive e-mail, organisations must have access to the correct hardware and software. Small companies cannot afford to buy equipments like a PC with a modem.
4. **Technical Issues**: In order to use an e-mail service one needs to have a certain level of technical knowledge. Beginners may find it difficult to operate the hardware and software involved.

8.1.2 Websites

A website refers to a central location that contains more than one web page. A website may comprise of one page or thousands of pages depending upon the need and requirement of the owner of the website. It is a collection of World Wide Web (WWW) files that includes a beginning file called a home page. From the home page, one can click on links to reach the other sections of the site. A website can be used as an effective tool for communicating with the interested parties of the business.

Importance of Website is as follows:

1. **Increase in Turnover:** Websites have a vast reach across the world, as millions of users access the websites. In order to increase its sales turnover, a company can use Website as a means of Advertising, where the potential customer can view the product features, colour, styles, graphics etc. which further leads to the decision of buying the product. Thus, websites becomes the tool of increasing turnover of the company.

2. **Build the brand:** A website helps to build the brand of the business. Website facilitates and gives unlimited freedom to determine how your business looks to your customer. Websites are flexible and can grow as business evolves and also allow business to be available around the clock, even during off business hours. It is one of the most cost-effective tools available for the businesses. Business branding through the web will help the business to develop a stronger reputation to millions around the world.
3. **To engage with prospective customers:** Word of mouth has always been the most trusted form of advertisement. Majority of the customers around the world say that they trust the earned media, such as word-of-mouth and recommendations from friends, family, above all other forms of advertising. With a website, it becomes easy for consumers to share businesses. With a simple link, they can instantly access all the information of the business. And with social media platforms such as Twitter and Facebook, it is now even easier for the people to share the things they love or recommend. Even business organisations can use these platforms to create the awareness for their product and company. Thus, the website plays a vital role in engaging the potential customer of business.
4. **Provide customer service:** Consumers can be educated about the business and can get answers to many of their questions which will help to cut back on the number of phone calls received by the business organisation with simple enquiries. Website can further support existing customers by offering information such as trouble shooting procedures, product specifications and parts list, how-to-proceed, diagrams and special help lines. By providing this help, available for 24 hours a day, one will be able to decrease the number of customer service employees.
5. **Global Presence:** Having online presence will enable the business organisation to compete with much larger and better companies. Websites have no certain place, no country; they are international. If the business organisation has a website, then they have something international that overcomes the limits between countries and long distances. A professionally designed website will give the business organisation an added credibility and visibility.
6. **Helpful in competing locally :** When the business organisation has a website, it gives a chance to the potential customers to compare the product with the competitor's product and subsequently help them in buying the product or engaging the services. If the business organisation has a professionally designed website, then it builds the identity of the organisation and thus helps in competing with the competitor of the product in the business.

8.1.3 ECS (Electronic Clearance System)

ECS is an electronic mode of funds transfer from one bank account to another. It can be used by institutions for making payments such as distribution of dividend, interest, salary, pension, among others. It can also be used to pay bills and other charges such as telephone, electricity, water or for making equated monthly installments payments on loans as well as SIP (Systematic Investment Planning). ECS can be used for both credit and debit purposes.

ECS Credit is used by an institution for affording credit to a large number of beneficiaries (for instance, employees, investors etc.) having accounts with bank branches at various locations within the jurisdiction of a ECS Centre by raising a single debit to the bank account of the user institution. ECS Credit enables payment of amounts towards distribution of dividend, interest, salary, pension, etc., of the user institution.

ECS Debit is useful for payment of telephone / electricity / water bills, tax collections, loan installment repayments, periodic investments in mutual funds, insurance premium etc., that are periodic or repetitive in nature and payable to the user institution by large number of customers etc.

ECS Credit offers many advantages to the beneficiary –
- The beneficiary need not visit his / her bank for depositing the paper instruments which he would have otherwise received had he not opted for ECS Credit.
- The beneficiary need not be apprehensive of loss / theft of physical instruments or the likelihood of fraudulent encashment thereof.
- Cost effective.
- The beneficiary receives the funds right on the due date.

ECS User institutions enjoy many advantages as well

Savings on administrative machinery and costs of printing, dispatch and reconciliation of paper instruments that would have been used as beneficiaries not opted for ECS Credit.
- Avoid chances of loss / theft of instruments in transit, likelihood of fraudulent encashment of paper instruments, etc. and subsequent correspondence / litigation.
- Efficient payment mode ensuring that the beneficiaries get credit on a designated date.
- Cost effective.
- Realise the payments on a single date instead of fractured receipt of payments.

Advantages of the ECS Credit Scheme to the banking system
- Freedom from paper handling and the resultant disadvantages of handling, presenting and monitoring paper instruments presented in clearing. Ease of processing and return for the destination bank branches.
- Smooth process of reconciliation for the sponsor banks.
- Cost effective.

ECS Debit offers many advantages to the –

Customers –
- ECS Debit mandates will take care of automatic debit to customer accounts on the due dates without visiting bank branches / collection centres of utility service providers, etc.

- Customers need not keep track of due date for payments.
- The debits to customer accounts would be monitored by the ECS Users, and the customers alerted accordingly.
- Cost effective.

User institutions –
- Savings on administrative machinery and costs of collecting the cheques from customers, presenting in clearing, monitoring their realisation and reconciliation.
- Better cash management because of realisation / recovery of dues on due dates promptly and efficiently.
- Avoids chances of loss / theft of instruments in transit, likelihood of fraudulent access to the paper instruments and encashment thereof.
- Realisation of payments on a uniform date instead of fragmented receipts spread over many days
- Cost effective

8.1.4 Writing a Blog

The word 'blog' is derived from the combination of the word 'web' and 'log'. The word blog is used to refer to a website that contains a writer's own experience, observation or opinions. Blogs typically focus on a specific subject (Economy, entertainment news, etc.) and provide users with forums to talk about each posting. In context of business, a blog is a collection of informal online articles that are either included in a company's internal communications system or posted on the internet for the public to read. Blogs are a feasible solution where the business organisations' have continuous information to share with their employees, wherein they are expected to respond promptly.

Types of Business Blogs:
1. External Business Blog
2. Internal Business Blog

1. External business blog: An external business blog creates content that is similar to a press release, only less formal. It is a blog where the employees of the company or spokes persons share their views and ideas publicly.

2. Internal business blog: An Internal blogs are often used to promote employee participation and discussion, to foster a sense of communication and to direct communication between various layers of a corporation.

Importance of Business blog:
1. **Keeping informed:** Blogs help in sharing business matters and keeping the employees informed about the recent business updates.
2. **Maintaining Public and Media Relations:** Company's spokesperson share company news with both general public and news journalists through their blogs.
3. **Helpful in connecting with the stakeholders:** Blogging helps in connecting and teaming up with the stakeholders of the company.

4. **Building strong network:** A regular blog posting helps in staying in contact with many individuals at a time. Moreover, every successful business organisation needs sound internal network. Blogging facilitate in making a strong internal network between various divisions of an organisation by a prompt posting of a blog.

8.2 Social Media Network

Social media is the collective term commonly given to websites and web applications that are used for discussion, debate and to share information online. The most common types are – social networking, blogs, micro-blogging, content communities, Facebook, Twitter, LinkedIn, YouTube, Flickr and Wikipedia, etc.

The need to ensure that social media networks are used responsibly, legally and with due regard to the provisions of other relevant council policies and codes of conduct applies equally to business, personal and private use.

In today's technology, we now transit the information through various communication media; we can use various social networking sites to communicate with the whole world. Teleconferencing and videoconferencing are mainly used in today's business world.

Sites such as YouTube see millions of hits a day, with online video and audio becoming extremely prevalent on websites. Business can capitalise by making the organisation's media.

With the rise of social networks, a form of crowd – based media known as social media has emerged. Business can take advantage of social media as another aspect of business communication, by performing such tasks as creating profiles on social networks, submitting online media to sites such as Dig, and using websites like twitter to answer consumer questions.

Sometimes, businesses need to make conference calls bringing several people together and technology can help here too. Programs such as Skype or Gizmo Project offer Voice over Internet Protocol services that allow individuals and business to call places all over the world for prices much cheaper than regular landline services.

Advantages of Using Social Media Network

Advantages of using social media network area as follows:
1. These sites give users a platform across the globe to express their feelings and views.
2. It helps users to interact with other users, no matter from where he operates.
3. These sites help users to organise and participate in any events.
4. Social networking sites help us to find our long lost and childhood friends and relatives.
5. It is a great source of communication between two users, irrespective of the distance between them.
6. These sites help users to refresh their mind and mood, as it is a great source of entertainment and gaming.

7. It helps to give some newcomers recognition in the world of music, acting, drama, and other arts.
8. Social media sites boost many organisations and business, through their promotions on these sites.
9. It helps to make people and the community aware of any issue.
10. It helps to bring social change in society.
11. Many people even can win many prizes through these sites.
12. These sites also help in terms of education awareness and motivations through many educational groups and communities.

Disadvantages of Using Social Media Network

Disadvantages of using social media sites are as follows:

1. One of the major demerits of these sites is an increase in criminal activities, as there is no hard restrictions on creating an account on these sites.
2. Another important issue is security of our personal data and information, as it is free to everyone; most of the users create fake accounts and misuse the personal information of other users.
3. Sometime some non-genuine and fake account users attack some religious communities and political groups.
4. It encourages pornography, and affects many children and youths.
5. These sites unnecessarily waste our valuable time, when the user spends time on these sites and get addicted.
6. Addictions of these sites can even affect our mental conditions, sometimes it is a big reason of depression and tension.
7. It also affects our health directly.
8. User's reliability is not sure; it is very hard to trust on any stranger on these sites.
9. At times it has been seen that it becomes the reason of one's death, as it becomes the medium to get in touch with the victim.
10. If affects the studies of children as they spend their valuable time on these sites and it adversely affect their concentration.
11. It encourages many scams.

8.2.1 Twitter

Twitter is a social networking and micro blogging service that allows you answer the question, "*What are you doing?* "by sending short text messages of 140 characters in length, called "tweets", to your friends, or "followers."

Twitter's bird logo

The short format of the tweet is a defining characteristic of the service, allowing informal collaboration and quick information sharing that provides relief from email and Instant Messaging fatigue. Twittering is also a less gated method of communication: you can share information with people that you wouldn't normally exchange email or IM messages with, opening up your circle of contacts to an ever-growing community of like-minded people.

You can send your messages using the Twitter website directly, as a single SMS alert, or via a third-party application such as Twirl, Snitter, or the Twitter fox add-on for Firefox. Your tweets are displayed on your profile page, on the home page of each of your followers, and in the Twitter public timeline .You can receive tweets by visiting the Twitter website, IM, SMS, email or via a third-party application.

Advantages of Twitter

1. **Helpful in Understanding Target Market:** Internet marketing can be done free of cost if the Twitter blogging service is widely used. Target market has to be searchedt and understood. One has to understand the needs and desires of the customer from their tweets, their passion and interests. Research can be carried out on the target market by following the tweets for better understanding. Strategies can be outlined for competitors as well by following their tweets.

2. **Effective Interaction:** Twitter blogging service provides assistance to networks efficiently and with large groups of people. Twitter and its third party applications permit you to segregate and interact with your target markets effectively. You can direct your Internet marketing campaigns at appropriate groups efficiently by using Twitter.

3. **Instant Communication:** Twitter allows you to communicate directly with your target market instantly. Normally, the process of communication takes time. For example, if you have a Website, the communication would be via polls, which are not personal or through contact forms which are time consuming and impersonal as well. With twitter, you can expect instant communication with your target market. You may have just posted a tweet, but a reply from your target market could come in an instant as well. Twitter helps you to gather real time intelligence from your very own target market as well as obtain valuable feedback. The speed of communication is just fantastic with Twitter. Moreover, your near approach helps to build lasting relationships as you will come across as a company that cares for its consumers instead of just hard selling.

Disadvantages of Twitter

1. **Spam:** Twitter is the number one site for spammers. One has to filter and weed out spammers from the lists from time to time, if one wants to measure the target market. Otherwise, the followers total will be an inflated number which will not help in Internet marketing campaigns. Filtering spam tweets is a lot of hard work. Other means of Internet marketing may seem feasible in the long run.

2. **Twitter is addictive:** It is very easy to get distracted when one joins the conversations or receive tweets outside the business interests. So one needs to strike a balance with getting friendly with the followers and meeting the internet marketing objectives.

8.2.2 Facebook

Facebook

Facebook is a popular free social networking website that allows registered users to create profiles, upload photos and video, send messages and keep in touch with friends, family and colleagues. The site, which is available in 37 different languages, includes public features such as:

- **Marketplace -** allows members to post, read and respond to classified ads.
- **Groups** - allows members who have common interests to find each other and interact.
- **Events** - allows members to publicise an event, invite guests and track who plans to attend.
- **Pages** - allows members to create and promote a public page built around a specific topic.
- **Presence technology** - allows members to see which contacts are online and to chat.

Facebook connects all your close friends together. It also maintains the privacy of the group by making it private. It allows the user to do group chatting, file sharing etc. It helps the people to stay connected.

Advantages of Using Facebook:

1. **Best Medium**: Facebook is free and it's one of the best medium for communication.
2. **Global Connectivity**: With the help of Facebook you can connect to different people from anywhere in the world, because almost everyone is familiar with the Internet and use Facebook. This gives us the opportunity to know more about their culture, values, customs and traditions.

3. **Appropriate to find Old Friends**: Facebook is the most appropriate tool for finding old friends. When friends go away to any other place, we often don't get the chance to communicate with them. But now Facebook gives us the opportunity to communicate with our old friends very easily without any cost.
4. **Sharing Thoughts and Feelings**: We can share our feelings on what's happening around us in our daily life through Facebook. We can also get feedback from our friends about their reaction towards our feelings. It is the best medium to share your feelings and thoughts with others.
5. **Helpful for Students:** Students can use Facebook for group study by creating a group only for studying. There you can share any information about your projects, homework, assignments, exams, due date etc.
6. **Gaming:** Facebook's online games are really popular and addictive. Facebook has thousands of applications, quiz, games etc. which keeps the user addicted with the site.

Disadvantages of Facebook

There are some Disadvantages of Facebook besides all these advantages. Some of the main disadvantages are:

1. **Addiction:** Facebook is an addiction for some people. Using Facebook for your need is actually good for us but when we waste most of our valuable time then it becomes harmful. The biggest disadvantage of Facebook is its addiction which causes many problems, mostly because it kills our precious time. Facebook addiction often brings adverse effect on a student's results.
2. **Fake profile and ID:** Fake profile is one of the major drawbacks of Facebook. Now it is easier to create fake profile with a stolen picture. People often use fake profile to harass someone they don't like.
3. **Lack of Confidentiality:** People can stalk you and get your personal information by using Facebook. It is highly recommended not to share your personal information publicly.

8.2.3 LinkedIn

LinkedIn is a social network in the world of social media that is accelerated toward business. LinkedIn social network is very common with those who are looking for work and trying to construct their network of contacts so they can extend to employers. LinkedIn is also prevalent as a way of promoting a business, because business owners can interact with those who are interested in their services by answering questions, participating in discussions and more. LinkedIn is the largest professional networking site available today. LinkedIn delivers a way to connect with other professionals and assist you to stay in contact with millions of users using a professional platform to keep in touch. LinkedIn is strictly used for exchanging knowledge, ideas, and opportunities and has increasingly become a leader in helping individuals find groups of interest as well as jobs in their field. As employers are increasingly researching people online, LinkedIn includes your education, experience, connections, groups, etc., and you can even include your resume, blog, and website all in one site. As a member of LinkedIn others will be able to find you even if you move or change jobs. Updating your LinkedIn profile keeps others abreast of what you're doing and what changes you are making in your professional life. It's also a great job search tool that can connect you with career opportunities, sales leads, and jobs. LinkedIn's Job Board shows who you may know at companies that are listed and can make it easy for you to connect instantly online.

Advantages of LinkedIn

As the largest professional network in the world, LinkedIn offers companies plenty of advantages. Like many social media tools, companies can use LinkedIn to not only promote themselves, but establish connections and build relationships.

1. Attract New Talent

LinkedIn company pages include a dedicated "careers" section that allows you to showcase your employment brand to those users who may be looking for new job opportunities. Under careers you can post job openings, but you can also do much more. With an upgrade to a silver or gold careers page, you can add videos and other recruitment tools that tell LinkedIn members more about your company, its culture and employees. The careers section can also be used to direct traffic to your website and Facebook page as a way of helping interested job seekers learn more about what you offer.

2. Connect with Top Prospects

LinkedIn company pages can help you attract new talent, but they can also make it easier for you to reach out to candidates that interest you. With a company page, you have the ability to find out more about your followers to determine who might be a good fit for your open positions. LinkedIn allows you to see detailed analytics about your followers including who they are and what they do. You also have the ability to directly message them and establish a connection.

3. Establish Credibility

Your company's overview on LinkedIn is your space to share status updates, blog posts and your Twitter feed to help followers and visitors learn more about what you do and how well you do it. A company page also gives you the ability to interact with LinkedIn members in other areas of the site including groups and the answers section. In both groups and answers, you have the opportunity to demonstrate your company's expertise by participating in discussions related to your industry and answering questions from other LinkedIn members.

4. Expand Marketing

Each LinkedIn company page has a dedicated section for you to promote your products and services. In this space you can provide detailed information about your offerings and provide links to your website for more information. To better target your audience, LinkedIn allows you to create custom campaigns based on industry, title, location and other segments. You have the ability to add rotating banners as well as coupons and discounts, videos, and recommendations from customers, peers and colleagues.

8.2.4 YouTube

YouTube is a video-sharing online public communication site. This site allows the users to upload and view videos posted by other users. It can also be used as an instrument by the business to communicate with the existing as well as potential customers. Moreover, it can also serve as in internal communication channel for the business.

Importance of YouTube

To start a business and making sure that it flourishes in to a profitable business are two different aspects. One has to put in lot of efforts to ensure that people view your product or brand. YouTube is one of the best possible instruments to put across your product or brand. The following are the importance of YouTube as a communication tool:

1. **To popularize your product**: If your business has a product in the market, adding an informative and entertaining video to YouTube can quickly get your merchandise in front of hundreds of millions of potential customers. If the company has a service to offer, you can use YouTube as a place to speak about the service, establish yourself and the company, can provide ways for potential clients to contact you.

2. **Internal Communication**: YouTube provides a convenient and easy way to use video hosting services; it can serve as an inexpensive way to post instructional videos, announcements and other internal communications with a more personal feel than conference calls. Videos allow you to demonstrate important concepts and product functions in much more detail than printed or verbal media.

3. **To receive feedback:** YouTube is a great tool to get reviews about the product as it has over 500 million active users. YouTube can also be used even if the business is not completely ready with the product. It can be the most useful instrument to figure out the response that the product might get. The company has to simply upload the video of prototype that it has made and it will start getting the feedback of it from around the world.
4. **Minimise workload:** In a business where the frequency of clients' call regarding problems with the product are more, then YouTube as a tool of communication can be a life saver and minimise the workload of the company. Here, one can avoid using his workforce to cater all the problems related to clients' call and can simply make a video with systematic details and share it on YouTube so the users can access it.
5. **Economic:** One of the most important factors in any marketing campaign is money. Conventional methods like advertising on television or newspaper require a lot of money, but YouTube allows you to upload your videos completely free, hence economical. From setting up your channel to analysing the traffic on your video, it costs you nothing.
6. **Prospective Opportunities:** YouTube offers a stage to make connections with the prospective opportunities as viewers of the YouTube are allowed to post comments on videos, and the company can provide them with feasible solutions, which build a new connection between the viewers and the company. Thus, YouTube is an important tool of communication for exploring prospective business opportunities.

8.2.5 Mobile / Cellular Phones

Mobile / Cellular phones: No matter what type of business you run, it is almost certain that telephonic communication plays a vital role in communication with customers and business partners. The mobile phone has become a part of everyday life for millions of people across the world. People now consider the ability to communicate by phone across the country (and even the world) as ordinary. Despite this fact, many businesses are still missing out on the huge potential benefits of using mobiles phones as a part of their business.

Advantages of Mobile / Cellular Phones:

- **Accessibility:** The biggest advantage of having a business mobile phone is that it becomes much easier to contact you. Instead of being told 'I'm sorry, the person is away from the office; a colleague or customer can be put straight through to your mobile phone. Even if they can only speak to you briefly, it is better than turning them away with no contact. Being available by mobile phone allows employees to contact you. In the event of a critical problem, it can be communicated to you and a decision taken, without you having to be in office.

- **Commonness:** Mobile phones are now so common that many people expect you to have one. Instead of hanging up when told you are not there to answer a call, many people will now ask for a mobile number as a matter of course. This is especially so if your job takes you out of the office for considerable amount of time. People will then expect you to have another number at which you can be contacted.
- **Time:** A mobile phone gives you more time to communicate. An important conversation can take place anywhere (e.g. on a train) which puts fewer restrictions on time.

    If you travel for three hours of every working day, then normally you would lose those three hours of communication. A mobile phone allows you to get those hours back. This means you can get through necessary phone calls quicker, and can provide better response time to customer or associate enquiries.
- **Details:** A mobile phone allows you to confirm and check details quickly. If you were on your way to an important meetingand realised you had forgotten a piece of vital information that usually you would be struck without it. However, with one call or text message on a mobile phone to an employee during the journey, you could get that information right up to the last minute without anybody else ever knowing.
- **Bookings and appointments:** Using a mobile phone has two advantages in the process of making and keeping bookings and appointments. Firstly, the ability to allow instant checking of appointments so that you can communicate with an employee, or with the person you intend to meet at any time to confirm, clarify, or alter meeting details (e.g. location, time).
- **E-mail message:** There is no need to go without e-mail messages on the move. It is now possible to be informed by phone call or text message of all (or specifically selected) new e-mails. Some packages also allow you access to all your e-mails via the WAP (Wireless Application Protocol) and GPRS (General Packer Radio Service) mobile Internet connection of newer phones.
- **Redirection and answer service:** A mobile phone can act as a good extension of a land phone. Callers to your land phone can be forwarded almost instantly to your mobile number if you are not there. For an extra cost, mobile phones can be used as part of an existing switchboard. This allows callers to be put straight through to you from the office switchboard or reception without the inconvenience of dialing two numbers.
- **Dual Lines:** One of the main concerns about giving employees mobile phone is that they will use them for personal calls and run up massive bills. However, banning personal use of the phones altogether can create a negative attitude, and show a back of trust towards employees.

    One solution is to use a dual line. Some network operators allow business to run mobile phones with two lines. One for business use and one for personal use

Employees can use the phone for personal calls, but pay for those calls themselves. This has two advantages. The employees does not feel mistrusted and can make personal calls when necessary; and the employers can be sure that they will not be paying excessive bills for non business calls.

- **International:** Most new phones are able to work in a number of countries, which means that even when you are abroad on business trips you can still be instantly accessible. However, the only problem with this is the huge costs. You are charged for incoming calls as well as outgoing calls.
- **Using Mobile Phones to Market your Business:** Small business owners can use the short messaging service (SMS) on their mobile phones to effectively advertise their business. The popularity of SMS can be gauged from the fact that in the UK alone, over 45 minutes text messages are sent every day, the majority of which are personal.
- **Using SMS to Advertise:** If you have a new product, service, offer announcement, etc., you can effectively target your customers by sending them an SMS. Most of the latest mobile phones allow you to send a single text message to multiple recipients. The only setback is that many of these phones have a maximum recipient number of around 10 (at the very most). In older mobile phones you would have to rewrite the message for every recipient.

Disadvantages of Mobile Phone / Cellular Phone

1. **Health hazards:** The radiations of mobile phones cause serious health hazards to the users. The mobile phone users are more prone to brain tumors, ear defects, headaches and blurring of vision. The mobile phones use microwave radiations to transmit data or more clearly they use these radiations to connect.
2. **Addiction:** Due to low priced services in the form of postpaid and prepaid the users of mobile phones can easily avail mobile telephony. Here the benefits get converted to disadvantages when the device is over used every time and at every place. The users of mobile phones are talking of the services, giving and receiving text messages; downloading wallpapers and ringtones and playing games. Consequently, they get detached with the other important activities which are so important for their social and personality development.
3. **Distraction:** The mobile phone user possess mobile with them all the time and everywhere. They take it along even in an important meeting. During the meeting if the mobile beeps and they get distracted from the important matter/issue that they were discussing.
4. **Bottomless Money Pit:** One of the disadvantages of mobile phones is the very fact that people are so fascinated with mobile phones that they are compelled to "upgrade" their mobile phones on a very frequent basis, looking forward to the second generation, Hi-tech and modern handsets. Such enthusiasts will want a

different phone next month, as well as all the accessories and peripherals that may go along with it. Cell phones can be a very expensive hobby, especially if they are upgraded more often than every two or three years.

8.3 WhatsApp

WhatsApp is a registered, cross – Platform instant messaging service for smart phones and selected feature phones that uses the internet for communication. In addition to text messaging, users can send each other images, video and audio media messages as well as their location using integrated mapping features. It is an ad-free mobile messaging app that allows users to exchange text and media messages through their Internet data plan or through Wi-Fi. WhatsApp software automatically compares all the phone numbers from the device's address book with its central database of WhatsApp users to automatically add contacts to the user's WhatsApp contact list.

Advantages of WhatsApp

- **Ease of Messaging**

  WhatsApp has created immense ease for those who text on regular basis. For several people, it has almost swapped conventional SMS System, by providing a platform that is not only fast, and convenient, but free as well making it cost effective.

- **Convenient Global Texting**

  WhatsApp is highly useful for international texts. A service that is often expensive on network carriers, WhatsApp makes it a seamless, cost free experience that helps you connect with your friends, associates, colleagues etc. on an international level.

- **WhatsApp Alerts**

  WhatsApp messages are displayed in little bubbles of text. Time stamps are displayed with every message and you even get to know through the last seen status, that the receiver has viewed the text/message. There are status updates, such as 'Available', 'Busy' etc. and background customisation preferences are available.

- **Group Messaging**

  WhatsApp can handle group messaging flawlessly. You can send a broadcast message to your entire list of contacts or can create a New Group, select the contacts, and send a collective message.

Disadvantages of WhatsApp

- **Hindrance to Privacy**: Even though you do not have the contact number of a person, he/she will get to see your profile pic, status (online or not) and can chat with you, if they have saved your number. This way people whom we do not like can start a conversation with us.
- **Addiction:** WhatsApp users have serious addiction issue, they are hypnotised and controlled by other users. They are so in to it that they cannot help themself without constantly chatting, replying and sharing all the time, regardless of the scenario.
- **Irrational Usage:** If someone wants to use WhatsApp in an irrational way, it is very dangerous tool to control the mind and trace the location.

8.4 Voice Mail

Voice mails are essentially digital recordings of outgoing and incoming voice messages that are managed either by an on-site or off-site system. Some users purchase systems that are operated and managed either by it's own employees or on a contract basis with another company. Home-based users, such as home telephone and cell phone users, often use an off-site service, such as their phone service provider, for voice mail accounts. Others, however, purchase software that allows their PC to become an electronic message system.

Voice mail system makes phone systems more powerful and flexible by allowing conversations and information to pass between parties, even when both are not present. In a work setting, customers and business people rely upon voice mail, both for leaving and sending messages. Outgoing messages e.g. are the messages people use to greet those who call their line. The outgoing message can tell a caller whose line they have reached, when that person might return and to leave a message. The caller, armed with this information, can leave a detailed message that's most appropriate for his or her needs.

As in the phone systems of old, many voice mail systems today come with an "operator". The difference is these operators are not human, they are auto attendants. Auto attendants guide users, both those from the inside and the outside, through the many options a voice-mail system has to offer. It instructs users how to enter commands through the phone's keypads.

Advantages of Voicemail

Voicemail is a computerised voice messaging system (more than just an answering machine) which can improve the client's service and enhance your productivity in the following ways:

1. **Reduces the Number of Telephone Calls and Callbacks (Telephone tag):** About three quarters of all first time calls do not reach the desired person. People tend to make far fewer callbacks, when they have a voice mailbox in which callers can leave messages. If a caller indicates the information they need and the call is saved, the return call can pass on the information rather than find-out what is needed.

2. **Reduces Holding Times for Callers:** Voice mail frees callers from being placed on hold indefinitely when the person they want is temporarily unavailable.
3. **Reduces or Eliminates Yellow Slips:** Voice mail reduces the need for message desks and live telephone receptionists providing an alternative to leaving messages (which can be lost). It frees administrative and clerical staff for more vital tasks.
4. **Available 24 Hours a Day:** Voicemail allows communication channels to be permanently open; it can be set it up to notify at any time and at any telephone number, whenever extensions receives a call. It enables to listen to and send messages from any tone dial phone in the world. Also if the phone is engaged voice mail will answer calls and take a message if the phone is forwarded to voicemail
5. **Reduces Interruptions:** If you are busy with important or urgent work, you can use voice mail to collect messages which you can attend to later. Studies have shown that two thirds of all calls are less important than the work they interrupt. Information can be provided in special announcement mailboxes.

Disadvantages of Voicemail

There are a few problems with voicemail that would make someone go anti voicemail which are:

1. **Long Pause**: It is incredibly annoying to have to wait until the beep comes along before leaving the message. First you have to wait for those annoying five rings to go through before the phone even sends you to voicemail. Then, you are told that the person you are calling is unavailable (as if you could not have already guessed that). Finally, you are told what to do after you finish leaving the message when just hanging-up usually is enough.
2. **People may not even listen to them:** There is no guarantee that someone has even heard the messages, or realised they had a missed call. Voice messages become old and nobody wants to take the time listen an old message. Or it may be that someone is angry at you and does not want to hear anything you have to say, which ironically could explain the situation and solve everything. There are many instances when a voicemail just does not go through.
3. **Poor set up**: Just the way you experience the voicemail set-up makes you despise it. For starters, having to use a password every time you access your voicemail quickly becomes redundant and annoying. Next, you are forced to listen to the voicemails starting from the first one, which can become a hassle if you have many messages and want to only hear the last one. Then there is the choice of deleting the messages; although this may seem like a savoir at this point, it completely becomes the opposite as you are told over and over if you want a message deleted followed by the same voice telling you it was deleted. It's never easy to get around the use of voicemail.

4. **Clutter Quickly:** If you are not up-to-date with the calls you miss, your voicemail could become very large. Listening to all of the messages could take an incredibly long time. You would have no choice but to listen to all to determine their importance, which could become more of a chore than anything else.

8.5 SMS (Short Messaging Service)

Short message Service (SMS) is a popular form of non-verbal mobile communication. Short message service (SMS), more popularly known as text messaging, developed as an initial by-product of the cell phone industry. SMS messaging is closely related to Instant Messaging (IM). IM is a function of online chat rooms and has expanded to mobile phones due to their ability to carry application that can be downloaded to the handset. The service allows for short text messages to be sent from one cell phone to another cell phone or from the web to another cell phone.

The Message (text only) from the sending mobile is stored in a central short message centre (SMS) which then forwards it to the destination mobile. This means that in the case that the recipient is not available; the short message is stored and can be sent later. Each short message can be no longer than 160 characters. These characters can be text (alphanumeric) or binary non-text short messages. An interesting feature of SMS is return receipts. This means that the sender, if wishes, can get a small message notifying if the short message was delivered to the intended recipient. Since SMS uses signaling channel as opposed to dedicated channels, these messages can be sent/ received simultaneously with the voice/ data/ fax service over a GSM network. SMS supports national and international roaming. This means that you can send short messages to any other GSM Mobile user around the world. With the PCS network based on all the three technologies, GSM, CDMA and TDMA supporting SMS, SMS is more or less a universal mobile data service.

Features of SMS

1. SMS supports several input mechanisms that allow interconnection with different sources and destinations of message.
2. With SMS, an active mobile handset is able to receive or submit a short message at any time, independent of whether a voice or data call is in progress
3. SMS guarantees delivery of the message by the network. The temporary failures due to unavailable receiving stations are identified, and the short message is stored in Short Messaging Service Centre (SMSC) until the destination device becomes available.
4. It is out of band packed delivery and low-band width message transfer, results in a highly efficient means for transmitting short bursts of data.
5. Additional services like e-mail fax, paging integration interactive banking etc.
6. Additional facilities like instant messaging, gaming and chatting.

Advantage of SMS

SMS provides benefits to subscribers as well as to the service provides.

- **Advantages to the Subscriber**

Some of the benefits of SMS to the mobile owner/ subscriber include:
1. Guaranteed message delivery
2. Reliable and cost effective communication device for concise information
3. Delivery of message to multiple subscribers at a time
4. Ability to receive diverse information
5. Convenient to use.
6. Seamless integration with other data and internet based application

- **Advantages to the Service Provider**

The benefits of SMS to the service provider include:
1. Increase in incremental revenues due to increased number of calls on wireless and wireless network.
2. Wireless data access for corporate users.
3. Additional value – added services like e-mail, voice mail, fax, stock and currency quotes, airline schedules, etc providing new revenues.

- **Disadvantages of SMS**
    1. They are limited up to 160 words only.
    2. They provide a limited text based experience.
    3. They can be very expensive.

8.6 Video conferencing

A video conference (also known as a video teleconference) is a set of interactive telecommunication technologies which allow two or more location to interact via two-way video and audio transmissions simultaneously. It has also been called 'visual collaboration' and is a type of groupware.

Video conferencing uses telecommunications of audio and video to bring people at different sites together for a meeting. This can be as simple as a conversation between two people in private offices (point-to-point) or involve several sites (multi-point) with more than one person in large rooms at different sites. Besides the audio and visual transmission of meeting activities, videoconferencing can be used to share documents, computer – displayed information, and whiteboards.

With videoconferencing people can interest as if they are talking face-to-face with both images and sound relayed in real time.

There are various types of videoconferencing, which is suitable for your application will depend upon the IT structure available and what it is that you actually want to achieve.

Videoconferencing has in the past been relatively expensive, but prices are coming down and it is possible for anyone with a fast enough Internet connection to operate a video conference.

Types of Videoconferencing

Videoconferencing can be divided into three categories of usage:

1. **Personal Video conferencing:** This is usually between only two individuals; yourself and the person that you are communicating with. However, it may also be between two or more people. Moreover, the videoconferencing system used between the participants should include at minimum, video and audio transmissions, and a dedicated video telephone or both. Other features, such as instant messaging and files transfers popularised through the use of MSN Messenger, Yahoo Instant Messenger, Skype, and AOL Instant messenger may also be included to enhance the experience.

2. **Business Video conferencing:** when face-to-face meetings are not possible, which evidently is the case in today's business market, the next best solution is through the use of business videoconferencing that mimics the atmosphere of business meetings or group collaborative efforts. Business videoconferencing includes most of the basic features as a personal videoconferencing, but offers addition resources such as:

    (i) The capability to include multiple people on the video call
    (ii) Collaboration features
    (iii) Document – sharing capabilities
    (iv) Enhanced presentation capabilities
    (v) Whiteboard capabilities
    (vi) Additional bandwidth requirements and
    (vii) Additional costs.

    Generally, business videoconferencing solutions are expensive, as it requires the set-up of expensive hardware, software, equipment, and a network or internet connection capable of a fast connection that offers professional results.

3. **Web Video conferencing:** It is a specifically used over the internet for the purposes of live meetings or presentation inside a web page or a class room type of environment between the presenter and the audience. Participants are connected to others in the web-conference via the internet through the use of a downloaded application or a web-based application where the attendees enter an URL to connect to the conference.

Features of a web conference may include:

(i) Slide show presentations.
(ii) Live or streaming video.
(iii) VoIP (Voice over IP).

- (iv) Web tours.
- (v) Meeting recording.
- (vi) Whiteboard.
- (vii) Text Chat.
- (viii) Polls and surveys and
- (ix) Screen Sharing / desktop sharing / application sharing.

Advantages of Video conferencing
1. Substitute for face-to-face communication.
2. Videoconferencing allows of people and individuals in different location to hold interactive meetings.
3. Communication is real-time.
4. Transcending barriers of distance.
5. Connectivity of different persons sitting at different places.
6. Saving in travelling costs of executives.
7. Saving in time of holding meetings and
8. Rapid expansion of knowledge of people sitting at different places is possible.

Disadvantages of Video conferencing
1. Blockage of space.
2. Heavy capital costs and
3. Not affordable by business houses of small size and scale.

Points to Remember

Internet is the largest network in the world that connects hundreds of thousands of individual networks all over the world. The internet in simple terms is a network of the interlinked computer networking worldwide, which is accessible to the general public.

Once a browser is installed, access to the Internet can be obtained through an Internet service provider (ISP)

Applications of the Internet

The following are some applications of the Internet.
- Email Electronic mail
- Remote Access
- File Sharing
- Social networking
- Marketing
- Education

Advantages of the Internet
1. Access to information
2. Information spreading
3. Communication
4. Production and commerce
5. Learning and cognitive development

Disadvantages of the Internet
1. Information Overload
2. False and Harmful information
3. Harmful Effects on Production and Commerce
4. Harmful Effects on Identity Formation and Psychological Development
5. Cultural Fragmentation
6. Loss of Privacy and Private-Public Boundaries.

Email or electronic mail is the process of exchanging message electronically using computers. Email allows users to communicate with each other in less time and at nominal cost. Apart from textual data, images and audio & video files can also be sent through emails.

Advantages of E-mail
1. Speed
2. Storage
3. Multiple Copies
4. Cost
5. Auditing
6. Multimedia
7. Flexibility
8. Group Work

Disadvantages of E-mail
1. Loss of Format
2. Security
3. Cost
4. Technical Issues

A **website** refers to a central location that contains more than one web page. website may comprise of one page or thousands of pages depending upon the need and requirement of the owner of the website. It is a collection of World Wide Web (WWW) files that includes a beginning file called a home page.

Importance of Website is as follows:
1. Increase in Turnover
2. Build the brand
3. To engage with prospective customers
4. Provide customer service
5. Global Presence
6. Helpful in competing locally

Electronic Clearance System (ECS) is an electronic mode of funds transfer from one bank account to another. ECS can be used for both credit and debit purposes.

The word blog is derived from the combination of the word 'web' and 'log'. The word blog is used to refer to a website that contains a writer's own experience, observation or opinions. Blogs typically focus on a specific subject (Economy, entertainment news, etc.) and provide users with forums to talk about each posting.

Types of Business Blog:
1. External Business Blog
2. Internal Business Blog

Importance of Business blog:
1. Keeping informed
2. Maintaining Public and Media Relations
3. Helpful in connecting with the stakeholders
4. Building strong network -Social media is the collective term commonly given to websites and web applications that are used for discussion, debate and to share information online. The most common types are – social networking, blogs, micro-blogging, content communities, Facebook, Twitter, LinkedIn, YouTube, Flickr and Wikipedia, etc.

Twitter is a social networking and micro blogging service that allows you answer the question, *"What are you doing? "* by sending short text messages of 140 characters in length, called "tweets", to your friends, or "followers."

Advantages of Twitter
1. Helpful in Understanding Target Market
2. Effective Interaction
3. Instant Communication

Disadvantages of Twitter
1. Spam
2. Addictive

Facebook is a popular free social networking website that allows registered users to create profiles, upload photos and video, send messages and keep in touch with friends, family and colleagues. The site, which is available in 37 different languages, includes public features such as:

- **Marketplace** - allows members to post, read and respond to classified ads.
- **Groups** - allows members who have common interests to find each other and interact.
- **Events** - allows members to publicise an event, invite guests and track who plans to attend.
- **Pages** - allows members to create and promote a public page built around a specific topic.
- **Presence technology** - allows members to see which contacts are online and chat.

Advantages of Using Facebook

1. Best Medium
2. Global Connectivity
3. Appropriate to find Old Friends
4. Sharing Thoughts and Feelings
5. Helpful for Students
6. Gaming

Disadvantages of Facebook

1. Addiction
2. Fake profile and ID
3. Lack of Confidentiality

LinkedIn is a social network in the world of social media that is accelerated toward business. LinkedIn social network is very common with those who are looking for work and trying to construct their network of contacts so they can extend to employers

Advantages of LinkedIn

As the largest professional network in the world, LinkedIn offers companies plenty of advantages. Like many social media tools, companies can use LinkedIn to not only promote themselves, but establish connections and build relationships.

1. Attract New Talent
2. Connect with Top Prospects
3. Establish Credibility
4. Expand Marketing

YouTube is a video-sharing online public communication site. This site allows the users to upload and view videos posted by other users.

The following are the importance of YouTube as a communication tool:
1. To popularise your product
2. Internal Communication
3. To receive feedback
4. Minimise workload
5. Economic
6. Prospective Opportunities

WhatsApp is a registered, cross –Platform instant messaging service for smart phones and selected feature phones that uses the internet for communication. In addition to text messaging, users can send each other images, video and audio media messages as well as their location using integrated mapping features.

Voice mails are essentially digital recordings of outgoing and incoming voice messages that are managed either by an on-site or off-site system.

Short message Service (SMS) is a popular form of non-verbal mobile communication. Short message service (SMS), more popularly known as text messaging.

Features of SMS
1. SMS supports several input mechanisms that allow interconnection with different sources and destinations of message.
2. With SMS, an active mobile handset is able to receive or submit a short message at any time, independent of whether a voice or data call is in progress
3. SMS guarantees delivery of the message by the network. The temporary failures due to unavailable receiving stations are identified, and the short message is stored in Short Messaging Service Centre (SMSC) until the destination device becomes available.
4. It is out of band packed delivery and low-band width message transfer, results in a highly efficient means for transmitting short bursts of data.
5. Additional services like e-mail fax, paging integration interactive banking etc.
6. Additional facilities like instant messaging, gaming and chatting.

A videoconference (also known as a video teleconference) is a set of interactive telecommunication technologies which allow two or more location to interact via two-way video and audio transmissions simultaneously

Types of Videoconferencing

Videoconferencing can be divided into three categories of usage:
1. Personal Video conferencing
2. Business Video conferencing
3. Web video conferencing

FREQUENTLY ASKED QUESTIONS FROM UNIVERSITY OF PUNE EXAMINATIONS

1. State in detail various Electronic Instruments used in Modern Communications.
   [Oct. 2007]
2. Write a detail note on various Electronic Instruments used in Modern Communication.
   [April 2008]
3. Which are the various Electronic Instruments in Modern Communications? **[April 2009]**
4. Write short notes on:
   - (a) E-mail **[April 2011]**
   - (b) Websites **[April 2011]**
   - (c) Electronic Clearance System (ECS) **[Oct. 2011]**
   - (d) Advantages and Disadvantages of E-Mail **[April 2013]**
   - (e) Advantages of Internet **[April 2013**
   - (f) Types of Websites **[April 2013]**

www.ingramcontent.com/pod-product-compliance
Lightning Source LLC
Chambersburg PA
CBHW062129160426
43191CB00013B/2238